STEPKIDS

STEPKIDS

A Survival Guide for Teenagers in Stepfamilies

Ann Getzoff & Carolyn McClenahan

Walker and Company, New York

First published in the United States of America
in 1984 by the Walker Publishing Company, Inc.

Published simultaneously in Canada by John Wiley & Sons
Canada, Limited, Rexdale, Ontario.

Library of Congress Cataloging in Publication Data

Getzoff, Ann.
  Stepkids: a survival guide for teenagers in stepfamilies.

  Bibliography: p.
  Includes index.
  1. Stepchildren—Family relationships. 2. Youth—
Life skills guides. 3. Adolescent psychology.
I. McClenahan, Carolyn. II. Title.
HQ777.7.G47 1984   646.7'8   83-21779
            ISBN 0-8027-0757-2
Library of Congress Catalog Card Number: 83-21779

Printed in the United States of America
10 9 8 7 6 5 4 3 2

To our kids and stepkids, who have enriched our lives as well as this book.

Abbe
Andy
Ken
Kevin
Mark
Rick
Rosalind
Tim
Ward

To David, for his good-humored constancy and loving support.

In memory of Pat, who believed in us and prodded and pushed us to the very end.

Contents

Introduction for Teenagers   1

1 * Normal Teenage Behavior, or, Driving
    Your Parents Up the Wall   5

Rebelling—why you rebel • Wanting privacy •
Wanting to be with your friends • Hang-
ing loose • Feeling moody • Getting angry—
knowing what or whom you feel angry at • Testing values

2 * How to Talk to a Stepparent   13

Sending messages • Assertive language: Why
should I say how I feel? • Listening • Two
more hints at good communicating

3 * Your Parents' Divorce   22

Why did your parents get a divorce? • How do
you feel about the divorce now? • Trying to get
your parents back together • Clever tricks that
don't work • Living with one parent

4 * Love and Remarriage   28

Different kinds of love • What you can do about
feeling unloved • Your parents' new marriage

5 * Everything You Always Wanted to Know
    About Stepparents   32

What kind of love to expect in your
stepfamily • It's okay not to love your stepparent • On the other hand, it's okay to love your
stepparent • Love can get all mixed up • What
to call your stepmom or stepdad • Stepparents'
pet peeves • Stepmothers' special gripes •
Stepfathers' special gripes • When your parent

and stepparent argue about you • Stepgrandparents, aunts, uncles and others

6 * Stemothers   43

They care a lot about what you and others think
of them • Stepmothers think they should be
perfect • Stepmothers believe they should love
you instantly • Stepmothers sometimes do
screwy things with their anger • Stepmothers
often feel jealous of their stepkids • Sometimes
stepmothers try to reform you

7 * Getting Along Better with Your Kind
of Stepmother   50

The stepmother who is basically okay but hung-
up • Mrs. Clean • Mrs. Smother • The stepmother who has no kids of her own • Stepmothers who favor their own kids • The cold,
rejecting stepmother • The secure and happy
stepmother

8 * Stepfathers   61

Stepfathers are not sure you want them in the
family • Stepfathers can be jealous of their stepkids • Stepdads feel competitive with your real
father • Stepfathers feel guilty • Stepfathers
feel like they have to be "superdads" to their own
kids • Stepfathers feel like a walking wallet

9 * How to Live with Your Kind of Stepfather   68

The Dictator • Mr. Grouch • The cold and indifferent stepfather • Mr. Hot Pants • The in-
visible stepfather • The stepfather who has no
children of his own • Physically abusive stepfathers • The stepfather who is caring and reasonable

10*Visiting Mom, Visiting Dad   80

Visitation • Feeling like an outsider • Step-family "jet lag" • Feeling that you don't have control over your life • Feeling disloyal and guilty • When the grass looks greener on the other side • When your parents use you as a messenger • When you don't want to visit as often • If your parents still don't understand • The advantages of having two homes

11*When You Don't See One of Your Parents   93

One parent says you can't see your other parent • Why your absent parent never comes to see you • If your mom or dad is mentally ill or alcoholic • If your mom or dad has died • If you don't see your sisters, brothers or other relatives

12*Stepbrothers and Stepsisters   103

It ain't so bad • Sharing your parent • Shifting roles • Feeling like an outsider and feeling like you've been invaded • The insider can feel like an outsider, too • Whose friends are whose? • Sexual attraction • Arguing • When you don't like your stepbrother or stepsister

13*Sex in Your Stepfamily   117

Living with a single parent forces you to recognize your parent's sexuality • Remarriage • Teenagers are often sexually attracted to their stepmom or stepdad • Sexual assault • Feelings between teenage stepbrothers and stepsisters can also be troublesome

14 * Parents in a Homosexual Relationship   132

   Why a parent changes from straight to gay
   • Feeling angry at your parent and his or her
   lover • Telling your parent how you feel • Will
   I be gay, too? • What do I tell my friends?
   • What to do about your other parent • When
   am I going to stop feeling so upset?

15 * What Is So Great about Stepfamilies?   140

Appendices
   I. How to Hold a Family Council   143
  II. Nine Ways for Stepparents and Kids to   148
       Become Friends
 III. When to Get Professional Help   153
  IV. Books of Interest for Stepfamilies   158
       • For Stepchildren
       • For Parents and Stepparents
   V. About the Stepfamily Association   161
       of America

Index   165

STEPKIDS

Introduction for Teenagers

We, the authors of this book, are marriage, family, child therapists. In our work, we talk with people—married or "live-in" couples, kids, and sometimes whole families—to help them work out whatever problems they are having in living together.

Several years ago, we noticed that many of the people coming to us for help had special problems because they were living in a family that involved step-relationships. The marriage was a second marriage for one or both of the adults and one or both of them were stepparents. Kids from the first marriages were either living with the couple or periodically visiting them.

Many of the couples were not legally married, but living together as a family and parenting each other's kids. Often they were not quite as traditional in their male-female roles as other couples. Although most of your parents were raised when men went to work and women stayed home to cook and clean, the experience of being divorced, being a single parent and remarrying has allowed these adults to structure less traditional roles in their new marriage.

Most remarried mothers work and many contribute more money to the stepfamily than do their husbands, particularly if the husband is paying child support to his first wife. Likewise most remarried men are likely to take on a more equal share in the household chores and parenting responsibilities. In most of the examples that we use in the book, the "he" and "she" could be switched and the point of the story would be the same.

We first became interested in these families because it happens that both of us are part of stepfamilies. We are both stepmothers to our husbands' children, and our husbands are stepfathers to our children. In our two families we have nine teenagers, so we know from experience that a stepfamily doesn't operate very well with the same rules that intact families use. ("Intact family," is our term for a family where the adults are the biological parents and the kids are natural brothers and sisters.) There are some very important differences between intact families and stepfamilies, and when stepfamilies are in trouble it is often because they have never thought about these differences. They are trying, in vain, to duplicate their first, intact family.

We couldn't help noticing that teenagers in stepfamilies have some very difficult adjustments, especially if the stepfamily begins when they are already in their teens. As a teen, you are old enough to have experienced most of the painful, sometimes ugly things that go on when couples are separating and divorcing; at the same time you are too old to accept a stranger easily as your "new dad" or "new mom." Sometimes divorce and remarriage are easier on younger children in the family. They don't understand as much about what is going on, and they adjust more quickly to change.

Because you have been around a while, you've been through a lot: the loss, pain, and rejection of a divorce; living with one of your parents and watching him or her try to be a single person again; and struggling to adjust to living with or accepting a stepparent.

You have had to do something with all the feelings and the confusion that go along with the changes that you have been through. If you are especially lucky, you have had at least one parent with whom you can talk quite openly about feelings and problems, and who gives you the time and opportunity to do so. If you are like many teenagers, though, you have learned to hide your sadness and have become an expert at pretending that nothing is wrong. If that is true, your feelings about your parents' divorce and remarriage may never have been resolved, and you may continue to feel rotten inside. Teenagers have a terrible habit of hurting themselves when they have problems and pain that they don't know how to deal with. Some kids decide that they are worthless or that they are somehow to blame for all the problems in the family. Some kids decide they simply don't care about anything. Sometimes they choose friends who are bad for them, get in over their heads with drugs, start doing poorly in school, driving recklessly, and in general treating themselves poorly.

In this book, we talk about many of the feelings and problems teenagers in stepfamilies have. Some of the problems will be familiar to you, and some will be entirely different from what you've experienced. The main thing we want you to know is that you can do some things to help yourself. If you are having problems getting along in your family, you are old enough and smart enough to make things better if you want to. The nice thing about being a teenager is that you have quite a lot of power to make things better in your family. Younger kids can't do that.

In order to get the most out of this book, don't try to read too much of it at one time. Look at the Contents page and find chapters that interest you. For example, if you have a stepmother who is so neat and tidy she drives you crazy, look in the chapter on stepmothers, where you will find a section about Mrs. Clean. When you find something that feels familiar, share it with others in your family. It's a good way to help them learn more about you when you may feel awkward or hesitant about telling them directly. Eventually, of course, you will go through the whole book,

and may be surprised to find that more of it than you expected relates at least partly to your own situation.

You might be thinking, "My friends are more important to me than my family. I really don't care about them."
Or, "I'm never home anyway." Or, "I'll be leaving home in
a few years, so why should I try to change anything?"
Those things are certainly true, but it sure is nice to have a
home where you can expect to find some support, some
love and attention, a good meal, or just a place to crash!

1 * Normal Teenage Behavior, or, Driving Your Parents up the Wall

Before we begin discussing stepfamilies, we would like to spend a little time talking about what you and other teenagers are like. If you are between the ages of twelve and nineteen, there are some things about you that probably make adjusting to your stepfamily fairly difficult, for you and for your parent and stepparent. Psychologists call these things "developmental tasks"—which means that if any or all of them describe you, you are perfectly normal and becoming an adult the way you should.

Rebelling

In order for you to grow up and become your own person, you will, at times, feel like rebelling against anything and everything that the adults in your family want you to do. If they want you to cut your hair, you probably want it long. If they want you to clean up your room, you are determined that it's your room and you'll have it any way you want. If they want you to be in at 12:00, you will come in at 12:05 or 2:05, depending on how much you need to rebel against what they say. The point is, you don't like them telling you what to do. If you always do what they say, you feel like a little kid, and you prefer to feel more like an adult.

You especially don't appreciate your stepmother or stepfather telling you what to do. You're likely to think, "Who the h—— does he think he is!" In anger you may have screamed, "You're not my father and you can't tell me what to do!" or "My *real* mother wouldn't treat me like that!"

Why You Rebel

When you rebel against what your parents tell you, you are saying, "Give me a chance to see what the world is like and figure out things on my own." Your drive to be your own person is at war with your parents' desire to protect you.

You actually started this process of checking out the world when you were about a year old and you touched the burner on the stove to see for yourself if Mom was giving you the straight scoop when she said, "Hot; don't touch!" Even then, you had to find out most things about the world yourself. As a teenager, your drive to be independent is much greater, so you rebel more. This can cause a lot of conflict at home, but it doesn't have to hurt you unless you are rebelling in ways that are not good for you. Cutting school so that you may not graduate, overdoing booze and other drugs, or driving when you're stoned, are actions guaranteed to freak out your parents, but by doing them you are messing up your own life as well.

Healthier ways of rebelling include demanding to wear your hair in a particular style, keeping your room as messy as possible, staying out thirty minutes past your curfew, and in general letting your parents know that you want to do things your own way.

This whole job of testing out the real world is much tougher when you have a stepparent to rebel against, too. Your little "REBEL" light flashes every time your stepparent tells you to do something. It usually takes a long time for a kid to respect his stepparent enough to feel okay about doing what he or she asks. Some teenagers we know try to tell their parents to bug off by having temper tantrums that would put a two-year-old to shame, when, paradoxically, what they are trying to say is, "Treat me like an adult!"

If you feel your stepparent is bugging you a lot, let him or her know that you are trying to be more mature, but that it's hard to feel grown up when someone's always telling you when to study or when to take out the garbage. It's best to say this at a calm moment and at the same time to offer to take some responsibility for household jobs *without* being told. If you do that, the trick is to figure out a way to remember the job so that your stepmom or stepdad doesn't have to start nagging again. Some kids write themselves notes and put them on their bedroom door.

Some stepmothers, instead of nagging, write notes to their kids to remind them of jobs, and the kids seem to like it a lot better. If you promised to take out the garbage right after your favorite TV show, then set the buzzer on the oven to remind yourself. (These tricks work with natural parents, too.)

Wanting Privacy

As you get older, you are probably talking less to your parents and more to your friends. For example, some kids are so into privacy that they don't even think they should have to tell their parents where they are going. But if you don't tell them where you are going, your parents might automatically assume what you are doing is illegal or immoral.

[7]

You can try to reassure them that everything is all right, but it probably won't help much. So you might try to explain about your need for privacy, and agree about what things they have a right to know.

If you do have a parent who can just listen to you without passing judgment or saying things that turn you off, you may feel comfortable confiding in that person no matter how old you get. Some teenagers tell us that their stepparents are terrific people to confide in because they are more objective and don't get as emotional as a real parent. But you have to trust that stepparent a lot before you can begin confiding, and sometimes that takes several years. Most teenagers need to have privacy at home, too. It is important to you to have your own room when possible and to have the door shut when you are there by yourself or with friends. Rather than screaming at your parents or brothers and sisters to "get out" or "stay out," you might try to explain to your whole family how important this privacy is to you. You can ask them all to agree to knock on the door and to respect your privacy.

Wanting to Be With Your Friends

Probably the last thing on your list of fun things to do this weekend is to go to Grandma's with your family. You naturally prefer to be with your friends, especially if there is a good party Saturday night. You may still like some special holiday times with your family, but a lot of kids only want to open presents on Christmas morning and split. Your parents will probably hassle you if that's the case.

If you were already spending a great deal of time with your friends when a stepparent came into your home, you may have wanted to pull away even more. Your natural parent may have felt hurt by this because he or she had some fantasies about creating one big happy new family, with you as an important part. It didn't occur to your mom or dad that teenagers don't want to be part of one big happy family with a stepparent whom they hardly know and haven't come to trust.

Hanging Loose

If you travel back and forth between two homes, you need to loosen the ties to each family even more. In other words, it's pretty hard to join right in and feel like part of one big happy family at Dad's house on Christmas Eve and then go to Mom's Christmas morning and fit right in there, too. Kids generally have feelings of loyalty toward both their families, and it can be quite confusing if you find you feel more loyal to your dad and stepmother than you do to your mom and stepfather, or the other way around. If they say or hint at negative things about each other, it may feel even more impossible to remain neutral.

You may find yourself withdrawing from your family and feeling rather quiet for a few days or a few hours before you go to the other parent's house and for some time when you get back. That is perfectly natural. It's easier to make those moves if you hang loose from everybody and feel like your own separate person. And maybe that's healthier for you, too, rather than trying to force yourself to be close to two different families.

Feeling Moody

"Mary Ann is so moody. She comes home from school in a terrible mood, snaps at her brother, and storms into her room in tears if I try to talk to her. Then, an hour later, I hear her on the phone laughing and talking to a friend, or she'll come and hug me unexpectedly in a very loving way. We never know what to expect from her," says Mary Ann's mother.

"Sometimes Tim is so selfish and inconsiderate I worry that I have failed miserably with him. Then I'll

[9]

learn that he spent an hour on the freeway helping a stranded motorist, or that he sent his last five dollars to 'Save the Whales,' or that he patiently listened to his little sister's speech fourteen times until she had it memorized. He's so changeable," complains Tim's dad.

We all have normal mood swings from joyful to sad, exuberant to depressed, loving to hateful. Teenagers just seem to go from one mood to another more quickly. New hormones surging through your bloodstream, the emotional stress of trying to become an adult, coping with school and your social life—all these make your feelings and your mood change from one hour to the next. This is perfectly normal.

Getting Angry

Besides being moody, many teenagers find that they feel angry a lot of the time, or it feels like they get angrier than they used to when they were younger kids. Part of the reason for this may be that anger is usually a second feeling; that is, it usually follows a softer feeling such as hurt, disappointment, jealousy, or fear. When we have one of those softer feelings, we feel vulnerable and helpless, like a little kid. Since you are struggling to feel more adult, you may find yourself not noticing the softer feelings as much and just going directly to anger.

We have noticed that the people in stepfamilies tend to have more than their share of hurt, disappointment, jealousy, and fear, so they are often troubled by angry feelings. If you are a teenager and if you are in a stepfamily, you have a double share, and your anger may cause you some problems. It is helpful if you can try to find the hurt or the disappointment and talk about *those* feelings rather than just blast someone with your anger. Sometimes you need to go run around the block or take a few deep breaths to allow your anger to simmer down a bit before you try to express yourself. We will talk more about ways to express anger in the next chapter.

Knowing What or Whom You Feel Angry At

One of the problems with anger is that sometimes we don't know why we're angry or who we are really angry at, so we take it out on the wrong person. For example, if your stepdad is mad at his boss and can't tell him or her about it, he may come home and yell at your mom instead. Stepkids and stepparents often feel very angry with each other about little things. They often don't feel safe enough in the relationship to express anger to each other, so they take it out on someone they are closer to and trust more, like their own natural parent or a brother or sister, or even the dog! One of the hardest things for people in stepfamilies to do is to accept their own anger and to learn to express it to the right person in an appropriate way. Family meetings can provide a safe way for people to express grievances and angry feelings to each other. (Appendix I, "How to Hold a Family Council" gives detailed suggestions for this.)

Testing Values

It seems that the way to figure out your own values—that is, whether it is more important to save the whales or buy a new record—depends on your testing extremes of behavior to see what feels best to you. You might be completely selfish one moment and extremely generous the next. Or you might hate your brother one moment and play a game with him an hour later. You might be sure you are going to college one day, but the next day feel like it would be a waste of time.

If you are adjusting to living with a single parent, a stepfamily, or two stepfamilies, your feelings and ideas about things are likely to go up and down even more. You may be confused about all your mixed feelings and if one of your parents asks you how you feel about something, you may say, ''I don't know,'' because you don't. Or you may say, ''I don't care,'' because it hurts too much to admit that you have some bad feelings or mixed-up feelings. This behavior is confusing to your parents. Since they don't know what to expect, they think you're hard to live with.

Now, add a stepparent to your life who doesn't know you very well, or maybe one who has never been around a teenager before. That person is going to be completely baffled by your behavior. She or he may think that because you are rebellious, messy, talk back, or object to being told what to do, you are bad or something is wrong with you.

We hope that reading about what's normal for teenagers will help you to feel more comfortable and will help your stepparent understand you a little better.

2 * How to Talk to a Stepparent

One of your important "developmental tasks" as a teen-ager is to learn to negotiate with adults. It is no longer appropriate for your parents to make all your decisions for you and to tell you what to do. In stepfamilies especially, it is crucial that you learn to talk to your parent and steppar-ent in a way that will make them willing to negotiate with you. This way, you can continue to gain more and more independence.

Sending Messages

Many times throughout this book we will suggest that you share your feelings with your stepmother or stepfather. We hope that by opening up communication some of your problems can be resolved. Unfortunately, most of us don't know how to share our feelings about something without blaming or attacking the other person, or using what we call "aggressive" language.

You are being aggressive when your sentences begin like this:

"You always . . ."
"You never . . ."
"Why did you . . ."

As you can see, most aggressive statements start with "you." When you use aggressive language, the person you are talking to will do one of four things:

1. Get defensive and try to explain why he or she did whatever it was.

2. Attack you back by telling you in no uncertain terms what you did first, or by telling you all about what you did wrong.

3. A non-assertive stepparent will look hurt, maybe start to cry, say you are right, in general put himself or herself down, and then resent you.

4. A lot of people use 1 and 2 together. That is, first they get defensive and then they attack you:

"I do NOT always yell at you the minute I get home" (defense) "and besides, if you did your jobs, I wouldn't have anything to yell about" (sneak attack).

So the problem doesn't get resolved and you say to yourself, "well, I tried to talk to him and he just won't listen," or "I knew I couldn't talk to her. She just doesn't understand."

Another conversation might go like this:

Mom: "Joe, take out the garbage, please."

Joe: (angrily) "I have to do everything around here. You never ask Bill to do anything" (blaming and attacking). "You expect me to do all your dirty work. Why doesn't your sweet little Bill ever have to do anything?"

Mom: (defending and explaining) "What do you mean you have to do everything? Bill does just as much as you do, and I don't have to ask him twenty times." (Counterattack begins.) "If you would grow up a little and take some responsibility around here, we wouldn't have this problem."

Joe: (storming out of the house) "I hate you. Nobody ever gives me a chance!"

When something like this happens, it's easy to make a little decision inside yourself that you're not going to say anything when you're bugged. So you don't—until you feel so angry that you say something aggressive again, and then you have another bad scene.

This works both ways, of course. The adults you live with don't know how to tell you what they don't like without making you angry either. Around and around you go.

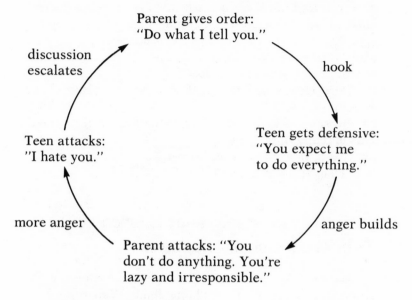

Parent gives order: "Do what I tell you."

hook

discussion escalates

Teen gets defensive: "You expect me to do everything."

Teen attacks: "I hate you."

anger builds

more anger

Parent attacks: "You don't do anything. You're lazy and irresponsible."

Assertive Language

It is important to say how you feel about things, and it's useful to learn to say it in a way that isn't threatening to your parent or stepparent. If you say nothing, you have only yourself to blame if there are no changes. And if you wait until you are angry and then attack, you get nowhere either. By the time you are twelve or thirteen you have the capability to learn to express yourself "assertively." You are old enough to begin developing some control over strong feelings, and you can talk about what you like and don't like clearly and calmly, in a way that doesn't offend the adults in your family. There are some simple, basic steps to being assertive.

[15]

Step 1. Good Timing

Don't try to send a message when either you or your stepparent is angry or in the heat of a battle. Wait until later. Also, don't come bursting in and expect to be heard until you find out if it's a good time for the other person. Make an appointment. For example:

"There's something that's been bothering me, and I want to talk with you about it. Would this be a good time, or would you rather do it later?"

Don't let yourself be put off by a "Not now, Bob, I have to go to the store."

Be sure to say, "When would be a good time then? This is really important to me."

"Well, how about after dinner?"

"Okay, I'll remind you then."

Step 2. Describe What Happened, or What Usually Happens

Be specific. Don't say, "You always blame me for everything and you never blame Jenny. You think that everything is always my fault." That's much too general. Try to describe exactly what happened one time.

Rick wanted to tell his stepmother that he feels she favors her own child, Jenny. He succeeds in being specific, but he makes another mistake.

"Remember the other day, when Jenny started that fight with me, and she was screaming her stupid head off like she always does? Well, you came running in to save her, like you always do, and started yelling at me, like it's always my fault. Poor little Jenny never does anything wrong."

If you can count nine or ten loaded words in that statement, I think you get the idea. Rick has attacked Jenny and her mother. I don't think he'll get anything but an angry stepmother.

Watch out for loaded words that blame or attack. Describe the situation objectively, like this:

"Remember the other day when Jenny and I were fighting?" (Stop and wait for agreement.) "She started screaming and you came in and told me to stop picking on her, that I'm old enough to know better, and you told me to go do something else. Then you left the room." Rick's statement was pretty objective this time. His stepmother can listen to him as long as he is not attacking her.

Step 3. *Now, Say How You Feel*

"Well, at first I felt hurt when that happened, like fights are always my fault and I'm a really bad guy, and no wonder you don't like me. Then I felt angry and thought that was really unfair, because Jenny teases *me* too."

When you say how you feel, be sure to use the name of a feeling. Some feeling words are:
- hurt
- jealous
- embarrassed
- left out
- angry
- disappointed
- rejected

Hint: It will be easier for someone to listen to you if you will use a "soft feeling" word like "hurt," rather than a "hard feeling" word like "angry." You probably got angry because you were hurt or jealous anyway, so try to say the feeling that came before the anger.

Trap: Some people think that if they stick "I feel" in front of anything they say that makes it okay. So they may say, for example, "I feel you were wrong." And they can't understand why they get an angry response from the other person. They might even say, "I'm only telling you how I feel."

"You were wrong," is not a feeling, it is a judgment on someone else's behavior. When someone judges your behavior, you get real testy, and will probably argue with them.

It is much easier to hear you say, "I disagree with you and this is why . . ." (which is a thought, not a feeling), or "I didn't like what you did," (a sort of feeling), or "I felt hurt and disappointed when you did that," (a real expression of feelings).

Why Should I Say How I Feel?

You may wonder whether you want your stepparent to know what your soft feeling is, because you may be afraid that your stepmother or stepfather will use it against you, or see you as weak in some way. If you are a guy, it may be especially hard to say you were hurt, or jealous, or felt left out, because you have learned that boys are supposed to be tough and not have those soft feelings. We know it is hard to take the risk to express them, but the fact is, everyone, male and female, young and old, has hurt feelings, jealous feelings, unloved feelings, lots of "little kid" feelings. People in stepfamilies especially have those feelings a lot; they are almost built in to being part of a stepfamily. If you take the risk of telling someone a soft feeling, you let them see you as a real person, and you are not quite as scary to them. (Yes, teenagers are scary to many adults.)

Jan is a new stepmother who was intimidated by her thirteen-year-old stepdaughter, Chris. Chris is a very bright girl who keeps her feelings to herself and appears to be cool and collected at all times. Her stepmother, Jan, is quite uncomfortable with Chris because she never knows what her stepdaughter is thinking, and does not know where she stands with Chris. Jan interprets Chris's quietness as rejection, and there is a lot of tension between them. If Chris would share her soft feelings, Jan would trust her more and they could be closer. You have to try it yourself to see if it works for you.

So far, we have suggested that when you want to say something important to an adult you will be heard better if you: (1) make an appointment, (2) objectively describe what happened, or what happens, and (3) say how you feel when it happens with an "I feel" statement. If you have successfully gotten that far, then you may want to go on with Step 4.

Step 4. Ask for a Specific Change

"I would like it if you would try not to judge whose fault it is when we fight."

Or better yet, offer a deal.

"I know that the fighting bugs you, so I'll try not to tease Jenny as much, and I'll try to ignore her when she bugs me. But when we do get into a fight, will you try to yell at both of us to stop, and not just me?"

Shortcut: The easiest way to use the ideas we have just talked about is to remember the phrase:

I feel . . . when. . . .

Remember to say a feeling word after "feel." When you can't think of the right feeling word, and "hurt," "disappointed," "jealous," "left out" don't quite describe it or feel too risky, try, "uncomfortable."

"I felt really uncomfortable when you wanted to hug me in front of my friend. I'm glad that you want to hug me sometimes, but I would like it if you could resist my magnetic charms when my friends are around." (A little humor never hurts!)

Listening

The other half of communicating with a stepparent is listening. There are going to be lots of times when your stepparent says aggressive things to you. In fact, lots of adults speak to kids in very aggressive ways. That's how their parents talked to them and that's how they learned to talk to you. It would be great if your stepfather could say to you:

"I feel so discouraged when I get home and every light in the house is on. What can we do so that everyone else members to help with this problem?"

Instead, he probably says:

"When are you kids going to learn to take some responsibility around here? Do you think money grows on trees? How many times do I have to tell you to turn the lights off behind you? Our electric bill was seventy dollars last month. Now who do you think is going to pay for that?"

If you are looking for a knuckle sandwich you could say, "You, dummy, who else?" But you probably sneak out of the room and stay away from him for a while, and think, "Boy, is he crabby!"

There is a way to listen to adults who are angry with you, or who are putting you down or asking you questions that have no answers like, "When are you going to learn . . . ?" It's a way that will keep you from arguing with that person and getting into a big hassle that you can't win. We try to teach parents to listen to kids this way in classes like Effective Parenting, but as a teenager you can listen to your parents this way too, if you really think and practice. What you do is simply tell your parent what you think they are saying or what they are trying to express, even though they did a rather poor job of saying it. For example, when Dad goes into his tirade about the lights, you say, "I know it really bugs you when we forget to turn out the lights. Maybe we can figure out a way to remember better. Got any ideas, Dad?"

"It really bugs you" is not naming a feeling, strictly speaking, but it will do. If you wanted to get carried away with this you could look him straight in the eye and say, "Boy, Dad, you must really feel discouraged when you come home and see all the lights on. You try so hard to keep the bill down, and we always forget to turn the lights off."

Your dad would probably faint dead away if you really did that, but you get the idea anyway. The trick is to keep yourself from feeling attacked and stop yourself from defending or attacking back. It will feel wonderful to your parents and probably improve parent-child relations in your house 100 percent if you could listen like this. Pick out a stock phrase to use like:

"It really bugs you when . . ."

or "You hate it when I . . ."

and try it out. These same skills, if you can begin to use and practice them, will help you communicate better with your friends, with the opposite sex, with your future husband or wife. As a matter of fact, good sending and listening skills will help you as an adult in whatever work you do.

Two More Hints at Good Communicating

1. Try to look at the person you are talking with (We call that eye contact.) 2. Try to use the person's name frequently when you talk to them. "Bill, there's something important that I need to talk with you about." If you look around at your friends, you will notice that kids who are well liked usually do those two things more often than kids who are not as popular.

Good communication skills are like being a good athlete: the more you practice, the better you get. Good luck!

3 * Your Parents' Divorce

How well you are getting along in a stepfamily depends a lot on how your new family came about. So, we'll spend some time in this chapter looking at your past.

Why Did Your Parents Get a Divorce?

First, let's take a look at how you felt and still feel about your parents' divorce. For some kids, having their parents divorce is a relief, but for most it's a blow. How you feel about the divorce depends a lot on what you were told or not told by your parents.

What did your parents say was the reason? Who did they say was to blame? Who did you decide was to blame? Your mom? Your dad? Or maybe yourself? If you're not quite sure, it's important to discuss it again with your parents because misunderstanding can cause a lot of problems.

Kelly

Kelly, who is now a grown woman, was only five years old when her parents divorced. She remembers her parents' divorce very clearly. One afternoon she was in her parents' bedroom while they were having a terrible fight. Her father pulled his suitcases out of the closet and started packing. When he was finished, he turned and walked out of the bedroom and out of the house without saying good-bye to either Kelly or her mom. Kelly decided (remember, she was only five) that *she* was the reason her father left, because he didn't say good-bye to her. She never saw her father again, but for the next fifteen years she felt guilty about his leaving. Kelly was one of those kids who decided she was to blame for her parents' divorce, and it was only when she could bring herself to talk it over with her mother years later that she stopped blaming herself.

Linda

Linda's story is a little different, but the consequences of what she decided about her parents' divorce are just as sad. Linda was thirteen when her parents divorced and a lot was said about who was to blame. Her father didn't tell her much, but her mother and grandmother told Linda clearly that her dad had been messing around with his secretary, Connie, and that Connie was the cause of the divorce. Naturally, Linda hated Connie, and her hatred got worse when Connie became her stepmother. Linda declared war on her stepmother, and their relationship has been bad ever since.

Very recently, however, Linda's mother began to be more truthful with her about the divorce and told her that secretly she (the mom) was relieved when Linda's dad left and that Connie was not to blame at all. At this point, Linda's relationship with her father and stepmother was very bad because she had "bought" Mom's version of what happened.

The point to be drawn from these stories is:

1. Be very cautious about blaming anyone for your parents' divorce. It takes two to make a good marriage and two to make a marriage fail. You do not have to choose sides.

2. Children do not cause divorce. Divorce is the sole responsibility and choice of the parents.

3. Try not to let other people's feelings control how you feel about a parent or stepparent. You have a right to love both parents freely even if they are divorced.

4. Check out your understanding of your parents' divorce. Feelings change as time passes, and your parents may feel differently now than they did at the time of the divorce.

How Do You Feel About The Divorce Now?

Now that you've taken a look at *why* your parents divorced, take a few more minutes and let yourself have all the feelings about their divorce. If you feel sad, that's okay and natural. Many kids have to experience their sadness many times before they can even consider having a relationship with a stepparent.

In some ways it's similar to the way you feel when you've lost a favorite pet. If your cat or dog has died or run away, you feel heartbroken for quite a while and sure that you could never love another animal as much. It's only after time has passed and you've had time to feel really sad about your loss that you can consider another pet without feeling guilty. Accepting a stepparent is like that. You have to grieve a while about your parents' divorce and your separation from one parent before you can accept a new parent figure in your life.

Trying to Get Your Parents Back Together

Another factor that can really mess up your relationship with your stepparent has to do with facing the truth. If you have not accepted your parents' divorce, you probably spend a lot of time fantasizing about them getting together again and having your life the way it used to be. To have these thoughts and fantasies once in a while is perfectly normal. It becomes a problem when you can't face the fact that your parents will not remarry each other. Until you accept this fact, it will be very hard to accept your stepparent. If you find yourself hung up in this way, you need to allow yourself more time to grieve about your parents' divorce—to feel all your sadness and anger at them for divorcing. It will probably help you if you can tell your parents that you are still angry and unhappy about their divorce. If you don't feel free to do that, get your feelings out in other ways: cry, beat your pillow, chop wood, hit a punching bag, throw rocks at trees, do anything that will help you get your anger out without physically hurting yourself or someone else.

Clever Tricks That Don't Work

Not too long ago, a group of teenagers was sharing all the things they did to try to get their parents back together. Heather said whenever she went to her dad's, she would tell him how lonely her mother was. "I know Mom still loves you," she would say. "Why don't you come home and give it another try?" Heather was hoping that Dad would feel sorry for his ex-wife and come back home. He didn't go back home, but he did feel more guilty than ever about leaving.

Holly said that when her mother's boyfriend called, she would conveniently forget to tell her or would get the message wrong, hoping they would get mad at each other. Eric said that for months he was as rude as possible to his mother's boyfriend and his father's girlfriend, so that they would both go away and his parents could get back together.

They all said that none of these tricks worked and that

some of the results of these tricks were very upsetting to everyone involved. Holly, who is now twenty-two and engaged to be married, said that as she got older, she began to realize that her parents had the right to decide for themselves what or who would make them happy. She said, "I finally woke up to the fact that my parents' happiness was the most important thing, because as I watched them learn how to be happy people, I felt happier, too."

Living With One Parent

After your parents divorced, your life probably changed a lot. Suddenly you were living with one parent instead of two, and that brought other changes. Some were bad and some were okay. The negative changes are easy to remember: missing your absent parent, perhaps having to move and change schools, having to help more around the house, your mom going to work. On the positive side, many kids find that they grow much closer to one or both of their parents after the divorce. Your mother may have been pretty open with you during this time: sharing her worries about money, talking about her job, and discussing her men friends with you. She really needed your help with the house or with taking care of younger children, so you felt very important and needed by her.

If you visited your dad on weekends, you probably did lots of fun things with him and spent time alone with him, perhaps for the first time. Maybe you cooked dinner together, went to the movies a lot, or just talked more than you had before.

This new closeness you felt with your parents was a pretty neat thing while it lasted. Most kids find, though, that this closeness disappears when their parents fall in love and remarry. John, a fifteen-year-old, described how things changed with his father. "It was neat when Dad was divorced. We'd go over to his apartment on weekends, stay up late watching TV and making chocolate chip cookies.

Then when SueEllen, his girlfriend, started coming over too, things were different. Dad spent a lot more time with her, and we had to go to bed earlier. I guess they wanted to be alone."

So when your mom or dad started to date and spend free time with a new friend, you went through another very difficult, painful period. We will talk about that in the next chapter.

4 * Love and Remarriage

Different Kinds of Love

This is a good time to say a few words about love. There are lots of different kinds of love, and many of us, children and adults, get confused about that. In your first family, it was probably pretty clear. Your parents loved you in a special way and you loved them in a special way. That's parent-child love. You knew that your parents loved each other in a special way and that was a different kind of love from their love for you. You probably were not jealous of their love for each other (at least since you were about five). In fact, their love for each other felt good to you. It helped you to feel secure.

When parents actually separate and get a divorce, love gets pretty confusing. When you live alone with your single parent and you begin to take over some of the jobs that your other parent used to do, you might get to think-ing that you are loved in the same way your parents loved each other. You might feel a little like a husband or wife to your parent. Then, when that parent comes home with a man or woman friend, you are bound to feel even more confused and jealous of the love that the new person is getting from your mom or dad. That jealousy might make you hate the new person a lot. That's what happened to Stacy.

Stacy and Her Dad

Stacy's mom died when Stacy was eleven and, since she was the oldest child, Stacy took over a lot of her mother's jobs. She cooked, washed, and did much of the housework for her dad. Although this was a lot of responsibility, Stacy grew to enjoy her jobs because her father was so grateful. She felt very important to her father and they became very close. This arrangement worked fine for both Stacy and her father until the time he remarried. Then the fur started to fly! Stacy's stepmother took over all Stacy's jobs, and suddenly Stacy felt she was no longer important or close to her father. Instead of being the "woman of the house," she was once again treated like a child, and she resented that.

It is important to remember that the love your parent has for you is *very* different from the love between two adults of the opposite sex. And when your mom or dad begins to love another adult, that doesn't change the way he or she loves you one bit. If your mom has a boyfriend, for example, it may feel like she loves you less because she is naturally going to spend more time with that new person and give him lots of attention. She may even act silly some of the time, talk on the phone for hours, and behaving in general like a teenager instead of an adult. That may feel confusing to you and bother you a lot, but it is perfectly normal, and your mom will act more like an adult again after a while. You may be getting less time and attention from her during this period, but it doesn't change the special love she has for you, and you are not being replaced. The same thing is true of your dad. He can love you in a healthier and better way if he is happily in love with another woman. It surely takes some getting used to, though.

What You Can Do About Feeling Unloved

If you are getting less time and attention and feeling unloved in general, there are a couple of things you can do. One is talking about your feelings to your mom or dad. If you talk to your dad, he will probably reassure you that he still loves you a lot, and try to explain the same things we have just said. If you need to be reminded more often that he loves you, you could ask him to do that. If you need more hugs, you can ask for them. If you need more time, you could ask for special time together. Your mom cannot read your mind either, and she may not be able to give you everything you need, but she can reassure you of her love. If you are feeling unloved, it is up to you to let your mom or dad know what you need in order to feel reassured of their love.

The second thing you can do is to spend more time with friends or relatives who care about you. Maybe you were spending too much time with that single parent and not enough with friends your own age. It is important to choose friends who let you know that you really matter to them. Everyone needs that kind of love, too; it works both ways. Learn to let your friends know that you care about them also. Some of the ways you can do that are by being a good listener, by calling people as much as they call you, by looking at them when you are talking with them, and by using their names when you talk to them.

Your Parents' New Marriage

It is worthwhile understanding that your parents' new marriage doesn't have a chance unless your parent and stepparent can learn to put each other first—even before you. Although this hurts you sometimes, and makes you feel jealous and betrayed, it is best for you and for your

(30)

whole family in the long run. When we work with stepfamilies, though, we have learned that it is not easy to the get the adults to really commit to each other and put each other first. This "couple unity," as we call it, was stronger in your first family, and is harder to develop in your stepfamily for two reasons:

Your biological parents had some time together as a couple before you were born. They knew and loved each other first. In your stepfamily, your parent's relationship with you existed before the new marriage. You've known and loved each other much longer than the new couple has, and your parent may feel confused about who should come first.

The other reason couples have more unity in a first family is because the kids are always rooting for them. You wanted your parents to be together and to be happy. If the marriage was painful and hurtful at the end, you probably felt betrayed. It's hard to have much faith in another marriage. You might feel this one won't last either, so you are protecting yourself from more hurt by not even hoping for a good relationship between the adults. You may even try to break it up, as we have talked about.

In the long run, however, you will feel the most secure when your parent and stepparent love each other, make it clear that they are committed to each other, and when they don't let you use your power to make trouble between them.

It may be hard for you to see this now, but living in a family with a happy, devoted love relationship is vital to your own growth. Home is the main place where you yourself learn to relate to the opposite sex.

Since your own parents were *not* very loving or close to each other prior to their divorce, one of the best things that can happen to you is to get a chance to live with and watch a close, loving relationship. You will have a much better chance of having a happy marriage yourself if you live with adults who are happy in their own marriage.

5 * Everything You Always Wanted to Know About Stepparents

What Kind of Love to Expect in Your Stepfamily

Most of us grew up with the idea that moms, dads, and kids are all supposed to love one another. So naturally when new stepfamilies are formed, the stepparents and the stepkids sometimes think that they should love one another the same way. The only problem is that love doesn't develop because someone thinks it should. Parent-child love develops from many years of physical and emotional contact, beginning before you were born. (If you were adopted, it began when your parents brought you home.) We call this contact "bonding," and the result is a very strong special feeling between parents and children, which exists even when they feel like they hate each other.

It's Okay Not to Love Your Stepparent

You and your new stepparent, on the other hand, are almost strangers. It is usually best *not* to expect your stepparent to love you like their own child, and it is important *not* to expect yourself to love your stepparent like you love your parents. If you like each other, that's wonderful. If you don't like each other, that's okay too, because you can still learn to live in the same house with some degree of mutual respect. Even if you and your stepparent like each other a lot, you may notice that she or he is not quite as forgiving of some of your behavior as your natural parent is. When your real mom or dad thinks you're being cute, your stepparent, who is more objective about you, may think you are being obnoxious. When your real mom or dad is admiring your assertiveness, your stepparent will think that you're being rude. A stepparent doesn't have that "natural parent bias" that your real mom and dad have. So stepparents often tend to expect a little more of you than your natural parents do.

On the Other Hand, It's Okay to Love Your Stepparent

If love develops between stepparent and stepchild, it usually takes several years, and is more likely to occur if the children are very young when the stepfamily is formed. Some stepkids really want to like or even love their stepparent, but they are afraid of being disloyal to their real mom or dad if they let themselves get close. It is important to know that you have lots of love available for all the important people in your life, and you are not betraying your real mom or dad if you love your stepmom or stepdad. You have the right to love both of them if you want to.

Love Can Get All Mixed Up

Sometimes a stepkid who has lost a natural parent comes to expect that their stepparent will replace the natural parent, and so they give love and need love desperately from the stepparent. That is what happened to Teresa.

Teresa, at age fifteen, decided that she wanted to live with her dad and stepmother. Her mother was mentally ill, and Teresa knew that she and her two sisters were not in a healthy environment living with her. Teresa's dad and stepmother agreed to have her move in with them. Teresa's mom got so upset that she completely disowned Teresa, told everyone she was dead, and refused to speak to her on the phone. Teresa really admired her stepmother, Louise, and the relationship she had with her two daughters. She wanted desperately to be one of them and to be loved by Louise in the same way. This was very frustrating and disappointing for Teresa because, although Louise liked Teresa, she did not love her as she loved her own children. Teresa could feel the difference and always felt she was being treated unfairly. This, of course, made Louise feel guilty and even resentful of Teresa's demands.

In counseling, Teresa found she had to grieve over the loss of her mother, and learn to adjust to the unrealistic expectations she had of her stepmother. She learned that she would always love her mother in a special way even if her mother couldn't love her back, and that Louise could not replace her mother. Louise learned that she could not replace Teresa's mother, and she actually came to like Teresa better when she stopped feeling so guilty.

What to Call Your Stepmom or Stepdad

We think familiar names like "Mom" and "Dad" feel most comfortable if they are mutually decided on by both you and your stepparent. Whatever you choose to call your stepparent should be comfortable for *both* of you. So unless you want to say "Hey, you" forever, you may have to bring up the subject. You should not feel obligated in any way to call your stepmom "Mother" or your stepfather "Dad" if you don't want to.

At the same time, if your stepdad doesn't want to be called by his first name that would be out also. Most teenagers prefer to call their stepparent by his or her first name, though, and this is usually okay with the stepparent. We've noticed, too, that when teenagers are talking about their stepparent they may call their stepfather "Bill," "Dad," or "My stepdad," using all three terms interchangably. Sometimes it's just easier to refer to your stepdad as "Dad" but that doesn't mean you necessarily think of him as your real dad. It's simply convenient.

Whatever you decide to call your stepparent, be sure to check out if it's all right with him or her. This needs to be done as soon as possible when you all get together, and since you don't know each other very well, it might feel awkward to bring it up. You might ask your natural parent to help you talk about it with your stepparent. If you get subtle or direct pressure from your mom, however, to call her new husband "Dad," don't agree to do that unless it really feels right for you. Your mom is most likely trying to promote everyone feeling close to one another, so you'll need to explain to her firmly that you already have a dad and you would feel very disloyal if you call her new husband "Dad," also.

Sometimes teenagers have just the opposite problem with the business of names. Patti, eighteen, has lived with her mother and stepfather since she was three. She's crazy about her stepfather and thinks of him as a real father. Her biological father, Steve, is quite jealous of Patti's relationship with her stepfather and has let Patti know over the years that she is not to call her stepfather "Dad." She does anyway, but then feels very awkward about how to refer to her stepdad when her father's around. The natural thing for her to say is, "My dad" this, "My dad" that, but she knows her real father would have a fit if she used that term in front of him. So she tries to remember to call her stepdad by his first name, Pete. That's really uncomfortable for Patti, as you can imagine, because she feels like she's denying the good, close relationship with her stepfather if she refers to him as Pete. In short, she can't win.

Some kids work that problem out by calling their stepdad "Pop" or "Pa" and their real dad "Dad." Others call one "Dad" and the other "Daddy." Some teenagers even call their real parent by his or her first name if that relationship was resumed after the child already was calling a stepparent "Mom" or "Dad." It really doesn't matter what you call your parents and stepparents, except that we do feel that everyone should have a different name. We know some kids who call two sets of parents "Mom" and "Dad" and refer to the others by first names like Patti, so they have to remember to keep switching depending on which house they're visiting. We think that is too confusing for the kids and puts too much pressure on them.

The most important thing about names is that your family is able to talk about them and tell each other what would be comfortable.

Stepparents' Pet Peeves

As we mentioned in the beginning of this book, there are certain things that a parent and stepparent can do or say that will instantly send you into orbit. The same is true for stepparents.

In fact, they're most likely to get even madder about certain behaviors than your natural parent would. There are two reasons for their big reaction. First, they don't have the same love feelings for you that your natural parent has so they are not able to overlook your behavior as easily, or see it in balance with your more positive qualities. Unlike natural parents, stepparents do not see you as God's gift to humanity and so are less tolerant of your screw-ups.

Secondly, stepparents are insecure about you and have a hard time trusting your motives. In fact, they sometimes seem a little "paranoid" because they think you're doing things just to bug them. This was the case with Mr. Wilson.

In the Wilson household, the stepfather, Brian, has the niftiest razor in the house. For a number of months, Tiffany, his stepdaughter, tiptoed into her parents' bedroom in the morning while they were still sleeping and quietly "removed" Brian's razor to her bathroom. If she returned the razor, Brian was none the wiser, but Tiffany tended to be forgetful. So often when Brian went to shave, his razor was gone, and all hell would break loose.

"Where is my #!=*! razor," he'd yell at the top of his lungs and Tiffany would sheepishly return the razor. Brian really got upset with this, but for some reason Tiffany continued to forget to return Brian's razor. It took her a long time to understand that this "borrowing" really upset her stepfather. To her it didn't seem like a big deal. After all, she didn't hurt it or anything. When she borrowed something from her mom and forgot to return it, her mom would get a little annoyed, but to her stepdad this same kind of act seemed like a major violation of his personal property.

So if you want to keep your stepparents calm, cool, and off your back, never, under any circumstances borrow anything of theirs without asking. If they do let you borrow something be sure to return it promptly and in one piece!

Stepmothers' Special Gripes

Criticizing her food and cooking. Most women feel very hurt if you make critical remarks about the kind of food they buy or the meals that they cook. If you absolutely can't stand something your stepmother cooks and you're sure you'll barf if you have to take more than one bite, be very, very tactful about what you say.

Borrowing her hair dryer, cosmetics, special conditioner, underwear, or clothes without asking.

Barging in her bedroom or bathroom without knocking. Knocking, and then barging in without waiting for an answer is just as offensive.

Eating her "special" food. Most stepmothers have all sorts of rules about food, of which you may not be aware. They may buy certain foods just for themselves, like a favorite flavor of yogurt to take to work for lunch, or other things that are special ingredients for a casserole they are planning for dinner. Stepmothers, like mothers, get very angry if they have to make another trip back to the market because you ate half the cheese they bought for a special recipe. Your best bet is to discuss this whole food area with your stepmother. Perhaps she can put all the "special" food on an "off-limits" shelf so you'll know what's okay to eat and what's not. Some stepmothers label food "Don't Touch!" If you have any doubt about what not to eat, ask!

Eating more than your share of the goodies. If there's a new package of Oreos in the kitchen, don't grab half the package. If you're starving, most stepmoms would prefer that you make a sandwich (provided that you don't put an inch of salami on it) rather than eat all the expensive goodies. Food represents time and money to stepmothers and they feel ripped off and angry if you're too piggy.

Bad table manners. Stepmothers usually have pretty high standards at the dinner table and get very upset if you chew with your mouth open, slouch in your chair, reach across the table, pile your food up in a big mess, and so on.

Not saying "Hello," "Good-bye," "How are you?" etc. Stepmothers feel hurt and rejected if you just slither in and out of the house without talking to them, or at least greeting them.

Leaving your stuff around and not picking up after yourself. You may be able to negotiate to have your room messy if you want, but your stepmother will surely expect you to keep your dirty dishes, clothes, and other junk cleared out of the hall, kitchen, and other common rooms.

Smelling sweaty. Stepmothers, like mothers, have sensitive noses and are put off by smelly bodies, hair, clothes, and rooms. If you come in stinky from a ball game, take a second to wash up before you join the family. If your room smells like a gym, open the window and air it out once in awhile.

Leaving your clean and dirty clothes on your bedroom floor. Stepmothers hate this because, if they are into gathering up your dirty clothes, it means more work for them. If you don't get your clothes in the wash regularly, and she stays out of your room, don't complain about not having any clean clothes.

Telling your stepmother how great your mother does something! Stepmothers usually feel pretty competitive with your real mother and are not happy to hear how wonderful your mother's spaghetti is, for instance, or how your mother got straight A's in college.

Stepfathers' Special Gripes

Borrowing their tools or personal possessions without asking or not returning them to their proper place. If you borrow your stepdad's hammer and he hangs it on the third hook in the garage, put it back on the third hook. Don't just lay it on the worktable.

Not showing respect. Stepfathers feel you're being disrespectful if you don't say "Hello" or "Good-bye" or if you "smart-mouth" them. Most stepdads were not raised with the same "freedom of speech" that you have been raised with. If your stepdad is not used to being talked back to or challenged verbally, he will NEVER accept you doing that. Most stepdads can't stand it when you talk back to your mother, either. He loves her and will get furious at you if he feels you are abusing her.

Wasting food, water, heat, gas, or anything! Most stepdads are pretty money conscious and get very unhappy if you take twenty-minute showers or forget to turn the lights out when you leave the room. Stepdads often feel like they are only a "walking checkbook," especially if they are paying child support in addition to helping to support you. They feel used and abused when you don't show some respect for money.

Borrowing the car and bringing it back on "empty."

Parking your car in his spot, or blocking the entrance to the garage with your car, moped, bicycle, etc.

Drinking his booze and mix.

Keeping your room like a pigsty. Men, and some women, feel orderliness and organization are very important and get concerned when your room is a disaster area.

Irresponsibility. Stepfathers cannot endure anything that looks like irresponsible behavior, like losing things, forgetfulness, or not considering others in the family. Because stepfathers have worked all their adult lives and have had a few knocks, they have learned how important it is to be responsible if you're going to survive in the "real world." So they're very big on showing initiative, keeping your word, and doing your chores—all the traits that go into making a "responsible" person. Most teenagers are not famous for being responsible, but if you're flaky about your jobs, your stepdad will feel he is failing you and that you will not make it later in life.

When Your Parent and Stepparent Argue About You

As we mention at other times in the book, it takes most people in stepfamilies anywhere from three to five years to get used to living with one another. During this time there's usually a lot of arguing going on because the people in the family are used to doing things their own way. This is especially true of adults who have very definite ideas about what's the best way to raise kids. If, for instance, you have a parent who is loose about discipline and a stepparent who is strict, there are going to be lots of fights about the best way to discipline you. If your parent and stepparent are having wars over you, it's very uncomfortable for you, to say the least. It may help you to remember that your parents are not really fighting about you, but about their differences. You just happen to be the focus of their different ways of doing things. It's also been our experience that married couples find it easier to argue about kids and teenagers than to argue about other things that are really bugging them (like sex, money, jealousy, or in-laws).

It is important for you to be as cooperative as you can be with both your stepparent and parent. If you are doing that most of the time, don't feel guilty when your parents argue about you. You're not a bad person, just a convenient battleground for them to work out their different values and rules.

Stepgrandparents, Aunts, Uncles, and Others

Most of your new steprelatives are able to accept you into their family without too much trouble. Some of these relatives, though, just can't cut it and are unfair in their treatment of you, or make it obvious how much more important your stepbrother or stepsister is to them.

Sometimes the relatives are unable to accept the divorce of their son or daughter and therefore can't accept their new daughter or son-in-law, let alone their stepgrandchildren. If that is the case, it is important not to take it personally.

When the Tilden kids first got a new stepgrandmother, she was nice to them, but sort of kept her distance and didn't try to make friends with them. A few years ago, their real grandma died, and suddenly the stepgrandma stepped in and started sending birthday cards, valentines, and doing lots of special things for the kids. It turned out that she was afraid to push herself on them at first and she didn't want to compete with their real grandma, with whom they were very close. She was afraid she would be rejected because they didn't need her. Then when the real grandma died she felt bad for the kids and their loss, and started to do things for them. They loved it, and they came to love her.

How to Cope

If your stepgrandparent or other relative can't accept you or is rude to you, they are limited by their own prejudice and that is their problem. Don't make it your problem, too, by assuming that if you were better in some way, they would accept you. Their feelings have nothing to do with you.

Be as polite as you can when you are with that person. Share your hurt feelings with your parent or stepparent. They can probably help you to understand your stepgrandparent's problem, so that you don't blame yourself.

6 * Stepmothers

It's hard to talk about stepmothers in a general way because, like everyone else, they are individual people, but we have found there are certain things many stepmothers have in common.

They Care a Lot About What You and Others Think of Them

Most stepmothers grew up with the same stories you did: Cinderella, Hansel and Gretel, and others that tell terrible tales of evil stepmothers. Everyone has some bad ideas about stepmothers, and your stepmother is terrified that you, your natural parents, your teachers, coaches, and your friends' parents will all think she's mean and unfair just because she is a stepmother. She definitely feels she has a couple of strikes against her before she even comes to bat.

Stepmothers cope with this "cruel stepmother" myth in a number of ways. Most bend over backwards to prove to you *and* themselves that they're okay.

Katie, a stepmother of just a few years, was very hung up on what her stepkids thought of her and was afraid they would hate her if she got mad at them. She explains her feelings: "When Ken's kids first moved in, they didn't know my personal rules about things, and I found myself becoming enraged over the most stupid little incidents. One time I found they had eaten some cheese that I had bought to use in a particular dish, so when I went to make dinner, I had to run back to the store to get more. I was furious, but I couldn't say anything because I felt so guilty about being angry. I knew it wasn't really their fault, and I wanted so much to be fair. But Billy, my own child, got to really resent being the only one yelled at when I was mad. He began to think I liked his stepbrother and sister more than I liked him. The truth was, I didn't like any of them much at all, because I was keeping all my anger bottled up. Finally, one day when I was screaming at Billy about something, my stepson, John, said to me, "It's okay if you yell at me, too!" I was so relieved, I burst into tears and hugged him! Now I know I can get mad at my stepkids and they won't hold it against me forever!"

Stepmothers Think They Should Be Perfect

A stepmother, just like any mother, wants to be the best parent she can be. But being a mother is a big job because it is usually mother, rather than father, who has the responsibility for raising the kids. Fathers and stepfathers see their responsibilities toward their kids in a different way, which we'll get into more in the chapter on stepfathers. Not so long ago, girls were raised to believe their most important job was to be a good mother. (Times are changing, but that is probably what your stepmother was taught.) Unfortunately, the measure of how good a job they do is how well you turn out. In other words, a stepmother can only be perfect if you are, so she may try to do lots of things to make you perfect!

Stepmothers Believe They Should Love You Instantly

Besides expecting herself to be a "supermom," your stepmother has another expectation of herself. She thinks she should love you right away. After all, she loves your dad a whole lot, so she should love his children, too. If she has children of her own, she makes the rule even more strict: "I should love my stepchildren as much as I love my own children."

Her love expectation doesn't work. It takes a long time to love someone else's kids, just as it takes kids a long time to love someone else's mom. Your stepmother may feel guilty because she doesn't love you yet, and she may even decide you are unlovable because she can't instantly love you. That way she feels a little less guilty.

As we've already said, you probably have some problems with this love business, too. People in stepfamilies often are pretty confused and guilty about the issue of love. When you think about it, it's kind of silly to expect people who hardly know each other to love one another. Your stepmom does know your dad pretty well because they probably spent hundreds of hours together dating, talking, and making love. But you and your stepmother don't know each other nearly as well and shouldn't expect to love one another for quite a while.

Both of you might feel very relieved if you could be honest with each other about your feelings. Talking about this issue is difficult, so you might want to share this part of the book with your stepmom.

Stepmothers Sometimes Do Screwy Things With Their Anger

We have already seen how some stepmothers can't get angry at their stepkids, so they direct that anger toward their own children instead. Another thing your stepmother may do is "displace" her anger onto you when she is really angry with your father. "Displace" simply means she puts it in the wrong place. Because she loves your father and values her relationship with him, she may be afraid to tell him directly when she is mad at him. She may even be afraid to admit to herself that she is having problems with her new husband.

So she holds her anger inside, gets real guilty, or in a bad mood. Then you come home and say something to her and WHAM, she explodes! She may snap at you and you think, "Excuse me for living," or you may feel that she hates you. Don't assume that you caused her anger. Rather than getting hooked into arguing with her, you might try good listening skills by saying to her, "You're sure mad at somebody," or "You're really in a bad mood this afternoon."

Stepmothers Often Feel Jealous of Their Stepkids

You had a relationship with your father long before he met your stepmother. You know lots of things about each other and have lots of common memories and experiences. You have the same ways of doing things and you value the same things. You have lived with the same household rules for many years together, and you love each other. When your stepmother is around, this special relationship may make her feel very left out and jealous. If your father takes your side in an argument, or tries to defend your behavior when she is angry at you, your stepmother feels, at

(46)

least for that moment, that you are more important to your dad than she is. You probably feel the same way about her lots of times, so it should be easy for you to understand her jealousy. You know that when you are feeling jealous of her being with your father, you don't treat her very nicely. And naturally, when she is feeling jealous of you, she is not going to treat you very well. Competition for love and affection is very common in stepfamilies.

Sometimes Stepmothers Try to Reform You

If your stepmother has children of her own, she has taught them her values, or the things that are important to her and her kids are probably a lot like her in the things they believe. If you have been raised by your own mother for most of your life, you may believe in entirely different things. For example, you may have been taught that school is your most important job, and that your school work comes before everything. Maybe your mother kept your room picked up for you so that nothing would interfere with your homework. Now, your stepmother may value children taking care of their own rooms and doing more things around the house. She feels it's your own business to take care of your homework and she doesn't pay much attention to it. That is a big change for you to get used to. Your stepmother may feel like you use your homework as an excuse not to do any jobs around the house. And of course, because she wants to be a perfect mother, she may try to reform you.

Tami was fifteen when she went to live with her father and her stepmother, Laura. Tami's mother had completely different values than those of this new family. She had had lots of different boyfriends around for many years. She drank a lot, and did not always choose the best men to bring home. Consequently, Tami had been molested a few times when she was younger by two of her mother's boy-friends, and she herself had hung around with some pretty tough kids when she was thirteen and fourteen. In fact, she had had sex with one of these boys when she was thirteen. Because of this background, Tami did not value her own body very much and she thought that she had to have sex with boys to get them to like her.

Tami was getting some counseling, and was learning to like herself more, and to choose more carefully with whom she wanted to have sex.

Tami had a boyfriend, and in fact, the two had a pretty good relationship. They got along very well and felt that they loved each other a lot. As you can guess, they also had a sexual relationship.

Laura found out about Tami's past, and felt terrible that these things had happened to her. She wanted to help Tami feel better about herself, but she simply couldn't ac-cept the fact that Tami had different values about sex than she did. And of course, she wanted to reform her. So she got Tami to promise that she wouldn't have sex anymore.

That was a disaster. When a teenager starts to become sexually active, she usually doesn't go backwards and stop having sex. She can learn to make better choices about boyfriends and about when and with whom she has sex, but her body doesn't let her just stop feeling sexual. It was very difficult for Laura to accept the fact that she couldn't reform Tami, that Tami wasn't going to be like her, and that she would have to value Tami, in spite of those differ-ences between them, if they were to have a good relation-ship.

Laura did come to accept Tami as a separate person with different values, but it was very painful and difficult. Laura, as well as Tami's dad, had to grieve over what they saw as the loss of Tami's "virtue." They had to cry and feel very sad, as though a part of Tami had died. Parents are very attached to their ideas about their daughters being pure.

Today, Tami is in college and doing quite well. She has

a very warm friendship with her stepmother Laura that will probably last through the years.

When you are trying to get along with your step-mother, it will help you if you can remember that she is a person just like you. She may act more mature in lots of ways because she has had more living experience, but inside she will have many of the same feelings you do. Even when she acts tough on the outside, she is often somewhat unsure of herself. She gets scared, jealous, has her feelings hurt, and has all the other "little kid" feelings with which you are familiar. When you get older, you don't get rid of those "little kid" feelings, you just learn to cover them up better.

7 * Getting Along Better with Your Kind of Stepmother

Stepmothers come in all different colors, shapes, and personalities. We have tried to think about all the different stepmothers we know and put them into categories. As you know, this doesn't work too well with people, so you may find that your stepmother is some combination of two or three of the stepmothers we have described. Rather than read this whole section, you may want to look through the chapter and just read about the stepmothers that are most like your own. We are hoping that the suggestions about "How to Cope" and "How (and How Not) to Say It" will help you figure out a way to get along better with your stepmother.

The Stepmother Who Is Basically Okay But Hung-up On Responsibility

This stepmother gets along rather well with her stepchildren, except in one area: responsibility. Maybe she wants to be a supermom more than some of the others, but she firmly believes that you must learn to be a responsible person in order to grow up right. She may want you to do your chores without being reminded, to do your homework right after school before you do anything else, to be home at a certain time, to be in bed by 10:00, and so on. Your dad may agree with her and support her on some things, or he may argue with her and defend you on other things. Some dads are afraid to say anything at all, which may make their kids feel like they're letting the stepmother take over.

How to Cope

You can get along better with this kind of stepmother if you are willing to take more responsibility. This means figuring out a way to remember to carry out the garbage without being reminded, folding the clothes before they get wrinkled, and doing some of the other small things that your stepmother sees as being "responsible." A little bit of effort in these areas goes a long way to getting your stepmother off your case. It gives you some power to negotiate about things that are more important to you.

If it feels like your stepmother is critical all the time and you're not sure what she does really expect of you, you could ask her to make a list of the things that are most important to her. Then you can try to negotiate with her about them. You might try to get your dad to join you in this talk, so that the two of them have to decide what they want from you.

How Not to Say It

"You expect me to do everything around here, and I'm not going to do it. I'm not a baby. It's my business when I do my homework."

Or, "Yeah, yeah, yeah, I'll take out the garbage, as soon as this show is over."

(51)

How to Say It

"I'm not sure what you expect of me. Could you and Dad sit down with me and all of us agree on what you want me to do?"

Or, "I can take responsibility for my room and for folding the clothes, but it would be easier for me to remember if you could leave a note on the table when there are clothes to be folded. Do you think you could do that?"

And, "I can remember to keep my towels picked up, and to take the garbage out every night, but I think I'm old enough to take care of my own homework without studying exactly when you think I should. How about if we make a deal that you don't say anything about my home-work this quarter, and if I don't get a B average, then we will talk about it again."

Mrs. Clean

Mrs. Clean is very hard to live with because it seems as though she has to have everything perfect—including her stepchildren. Her main concern, though, is the house, which she wants spotless at all times. Dishes can never be left in the sink, the tub is to be cleaned after every bath, and the pillows on the sofa have to be arranged just so. A stepmother we know even insisted that her stepchildren take off their shoes the moment they came into the house so they wouldn't track in dirt. Instead of greeting her kids with a "Hi, how was school?," she generally greeted them with "Take your shoes off, don't put your books there, don't mess up the kitchen . . ."

Kids living with Mrs. Clean are very uncomfortable in their own home, and don't want to bring their friends home because it's not a very relaxing place. Getting this kind of stepmother to stop being so uptight about the house is not easy. Women like this feel very guilty when their houses aren't perfect, so you're fighting a powerful emotion: guilt. There are some things you can do, nevertheless.

How to Cope

First, tell your stepmom that you are very unhappy trying to live up to her standards of cleanliness. Choose a few things that bug you the most and see if she will change the rules for those things. For instance, if you and your friends are never allowed in the living room, ask to be given a chance to take one or two friends in there, just to talk or listen to music, so that your stepmother can see that you won't destroy the place.

Again, see if you can get your stepmom and your dad to agree on some house rules, to write them down and the discuss them with you.

During the discussion of the rules, try to compromise. For instance, your stepmother may be willing to make a deal with you about your bedroom. It usually goes like this: you agree to clean your room once a week (pick up your clothes, vacuum, dust, get rid of the banana peels), and your stepmom agrees to let your room be the way you want it the rest of the time. Part of the deal is that you keep your bedroom door closed so your stepmom won't have to look at the mess!

How Not to Say It

"You're too picky. It's my room and I'll keep it any way I want it."

How to Say It

"I'm having a very hard time living up to your standards. The thing that is hardest for me is to keep my room as clean as you want it all the time. Could we work out a

deal about that? I really like it kind of messy, but I'm willing to compromise with you.""

Mrs. Smother

This kind of stepmother means well but drives her stepkids nuts because she wants to be too involved with their
lives. She wants you to talk with her about everything. She
is always there when you get home, asking about school
and trying to engage you and your friends in conversation,
and she frequently comes into your room to talk when you
really want to be alone. She wants to make your decisions
for you and, in general, treats you as if you were five years
old. She may also embarrass you because she's too affectionate.

How to Cope

First, let's take the issue of affection. You don't want
to hurt your stepmother's feelings, but somehow, you
want her to stop what she's doing. A good way to approach
her on this issue is to tell her that you appreciate her
warm feelings toward you, but that you find her affection
kind of uncomfortable. Be real specific about what's okay
and what's not okay. For example, it may be okay if she
gives you a light kiss on the cheek when your friends
aren't around, but not when they're there! Or you may be
comfortable with a pat on the back but loathe being
kissed. Since your stepmother is a warm kind of person,
it's nice to give her some clues about how she can express
her affection without turning her off completely.
    If you find your stepmother too nosy about what you
consider to be your business, use the same technique you
used with affection. Tell her what kinds of things you are
willing to talk to her about and what things are off limits.
For example, you may not want to tell her a thing about

your dates, other than where you went, but are comfortable talking about your soccer game. Your stepmother wants a good relationship with you and probably doesn't realize she's trying to get too close. If you have been trying to cope by withdrawing, avoiding her, or being rude, she has probably tried even harder to be your friend. In the long run it will be easier if you talk with her about it.

How Not to Say It

"Will you butt out of my business!"
"Stop being so —— nosy!
"Do you *have* to kiss me all the time?"

How to Say It

"I really get embarrassed when you want to hug or kiss me in front of my friends."
"I don't mind telling you about my game, or what movie I saw, but what I did on my date is sort of private and I don't like you to ask about it."

The Stepmother Who Has No Kids of Her Own

This is a tough situation for both your stepmother and you. Although this may not show, stepmothers who have never had children are usually very unsure of themselves. She's not sure what's fair to expect from you and she's not sure how to treat you. Sometimes she may not be much older than you and may feel really confused about how to be a mom to you. These stepmothers tend to expect too much from you, and are blown away by how messy, irresponsible, and mouthy you are. Your stepmother may

(55)

think you are abnormal when, in fact, you're probably about average.

How to Cope

You need to be really straight with your stepmother about your feelings. You can tell her, as kindly as possible, that she expects too much of you and that you feel put down and criticized most of the time.

Never borrow her personal possessions without asking.

Try to negotiate with her about specific things that bug each of you.

Encourage your stepmother to go to activities in which you are involved, like school plays, basketball games, school meetings, etc. There she will meet other mothers and find out about other kids and their parents. If you decide to talk to your stepmom about changing things, you may have better luck if you don't include your dad in the conversation. This is especially true if your dad is pretty much on your side but doesn't want to hurt his wife. The chances are pretty good that your dad and stepmother have had plenty of disagreements about your behavior. Your stepmother will feel more defensive and not listen well if you both talk to her at the same time. To her it will seem like two against one!

How Not to Say It

"Boy, you don't know a thing about kids!"

"You just want me to be perfect like you were when you were a kid."

How to Say It

"I really try to keep my stuff picked up, but most of the time I have other things on my mind. I'm no different

[56]

from my friends, but I feel like you expect me to be an adult all the time, and I can't be."

Stepmothers Who Favor Their Own Kids

What we are talking about here is not the stepmother who is unfair once in a while, but the kind who always treats her own children better than her stepchildren. This is the kind of stepmother Cinderella had. She may give her own kids more expensive presents, or let her own kids get away with murder, but come down hard on you if you do the same thing. In short, she is not fair.

How to Cope

In this situation, as in the others we've talked about, if you want something to change you have to take the risk of talking to your stepmother about your feelings. This should be done when neither of you is angry, so you'll be able to listen to one another. Be specific about your complaints.

If your stepmother seems to be angry at your father a lot, it may be that she is taking out that anger on you. You might try to tell her that you feel like she is angry at you all the time, and you don't know what you did to make her feel that way.

Don't blame your stepbrothers and sisters because your stepmother is unfair. It's natural to feel angry at them when they get a better deal than you, but try to remember, they are not to blame. Like all kids, they will take advantage of a situation if someone lets them. Also, you will probably be the stronger, more independent adult for not being the favored child. Just remember, you are really angry at your stepmother, not at the other kids in the family.

If all these ideas fail, do your best to accept the situation. If you expect your stepmother to be unfair and to treat her own kids better than you, you will not be quite as disappointed when she does. You will need to tell yourself that it is her problem and there is nothing wrong with you just because she can't appreciate you. Look to other adults who do appreciate and like you and spend time with them in order to keep feeling good about yourself.

How Not to Say It

"You always pick on me."

"Oh yeah, *your* kids are just perfect."

How to Say It

"When Sue leaves her stuff all over the house, you don't seem to mind, or you even pick it up, but when I do the same thing you get real upset."

The Cold, Rejecting Stepmother

Fortunately, there are not many women like this, but a few are just not capable of loving or accepting any child. Frieda Winter is a good example. She had two children of her own whom she hadn't seen since her divorce from their father years ago. Eventually, she married a man who had a seven-year-old son, Eddie. Frieda had only met Eddie twice before she married Eddie's dad and they began living together as a family. Frieda decided she hated Eddie. She often told Eddie how much she loathed him and couldn't wait until Eddie grew up and got out of the house. She was never affectionate to Eddie, and often slapped him. Eddie had lived in this grim household for eight years, until recently, when Frieda and Eddie's dad were separated.

The small number of women who are like this have many, many problems of their own. They are not capable of loving children, or anyone, because they were not loved as children either. The person they always hate most is themselves.

How to Cope

If you are really being treated this badly by your stepmother, this may be one situation where you need to talk with your father about how unhappy you are. Between the two of you, you may be able to figure out a more comfortable way to live with your stepmother.

If your dad can't support you or help you, talk to your school counselor or a teacher you like and trust. Another adult may be able to help your parents understand how bad it is for you to live in a situation where someone dislikes you. Perhaps your school counselor can encourage your parents to go to a family counselor.

If you often think of running away, you should probably try to find someplace else to live. Do you have a grandmother, uncle, cousin, or friend with whom you could live? If no relatives are available to you, ask your school counselor to help you find out about foster homes.

The Secure and Happy Stepmother

This stepmother has a good relationship with her husband and also with her stepchildren. She is accepting of her stepkids, is warm and friendly toward them, and she doesn't have to be a "supermom" as much as some of the other stepmothers. When she disciplines, she doesn't get carried away. She is able to express her feelings about things clearly and directly. She can get angry at her stepkids and at her husband, and she knows at whom she's mad. This woman is quite mature, and probably has a full life in every respect. She has a few close friends and a career or interest that is really important to her. She does not get overinvolved in the lives of her children or stepchildren.

It is important to say that the stepmothers we know who are like this have been in stepfamilies for at least two or three years. That's usually how long it takes most women to feel relaxed and confident in a stepfamily. If you have a stepmother like this, what you need to say is, "Boy, am I lucky!"

8 * Stepfathers

Although stepfathers can be very different from one another, we've found that, just like stepmothers, they have certain feelings in common.

Stepfathers Have No Idea What They Are Getting Into (or, Love Is Blind)

Before your stepfather married your mother, he thought it would be fairly easy to become a part of your family. He knew there would be some problems, but he was blind to how complex they would be. He thought that his love for your mother would conquer all. If he was married before, this marriage seemed to him like a second chance for happiness. After the honeymoon, reality began to settle in, and he realized how difficult it is to blend into a new family. He found it especially hard to form good relationships with you and any other kids in the family, and at the same time maintain his relationship with his own kids, if he has any. He didn't realize for example, that if you had a good relationship with your real father, he would feel that he had to live up to that. On the other hand, if you had a bad relationship with your father, you may not want to relate to your stepfather much at all. If your real father died, you may have an ideal picture of him, and your stepfather may seem pretty ordinary in comparison. In other words, he can't win! After a few months, your stepfather probably felt some disappointment in himself and in you, as it was probably much harder to get something going with you than he thought it would be. Stepfathers often have the fear that they will fail as a husband and father.

Stepfathers Are Not Sure You Want Them in the Family

When you found out your mom was going to get married again, you probably felt several things all at the same time. On one hand, you were pleased that Mom was happy, but at the same time, you were concerned about where you would fit in when Mr. Wonderful moved in.

A new stepfather has similar feelings. When he marries a woman who has children, he is often not sure he will be accepted. It appears that his wife and her children are a tight unit and he is not really sure if there is room for him, too. His stepkids and wife have lived together for many years and shared thousands of experiences. He is quite concerned about being accepted as part of this family. One new stepdad put it this way, "I'm not sure what my stepson wants of me. I want him to consider me part of his family—not necessarily his father, but part of his family. But when I say, 'our family,' my stepson says, 'You're not part of my family.'"

Stepfathers Can Be Jealous of Their Stepkids

When a stepdad begins to live with his new wife and step-children, he finds that he has to share his wife with her kids. Some men feel okay about sharing but many feel pretty darn jealous of the time and attention their wives give the kids, just as you may resent the time your mom spends with your stepdad. Jerry, a stepdad we know, said his competitive feelings were strongest when he first came home from work at night.

"I really looked forward to seeing Sherry and talking with her. She would sit on the bed and talk with me while I changed my clothes, and that was a very special time for me. But my four-year-old stepdaughter, Rose, would always come running in or call, 'Mommie, Mommie,' and Sherry would interrupt our conversation to talk to her or see what she wanted. I really resented that. After all, Rose had all day to talk to her mother."

Stepdads Feel Competitive With Your Real Father

Although it's hard for many stepfathers to talk about, they often feel very competitive with your real dad. Some feel they are in a contest with your dad to see who you like the best. Rhonda's stepdad was like this. When Rhonda was three, her mother married a man named Bob. Bob was very fond of Rhonda but found himself being pretty distant with her. Rhonda thought her real father was wonderful, and Bob didn't think he had a chance in winning her love. He acted cool toward her until she was about twelve. Suddenly, Rhonda began seeing and saying negative things about her real father. It was only then that Bob allowed himself to get closer to her and more involved in her life. He was no longer so afraid that Rhonda would reject him in favor of her real father.

Stepfathers try to keep these competitive feelings quiet because they're embarrassed by them and feel they're childish. Those feelings are very strong, however, and it may be that your stepfather is keeping his distance because he feels he can't compete with your real dad.

Some stepdads try to win their stepkids' love by putting down the kids' real father. When stepdads do this they are really saying, "Your dad's a jerk, so you should love and appreciate me. See how good I am in comparison to your real dad?"

If it seems like your stepdad is jealous of your real dad and often puts him down, there are some things you can do to help the situation a little:

1. When you are feeling good about your stepdad, tell him that. You don't have to make a big production about it but you can say something like, "Thanks for helping me with my homework." He'll feel appreciated by you and will probably not feel like such a loser in comparison to your real dad.

2. Tell your stepdad that you feel pretty upset when he puts down your real father. You could say, "It's hard for me when you say things about my dad. I want to defend him, and even if I don't say anything, I wind up feeling mad at you."

Or, "It feels like it's not okay with you if I love my dad. I know Dad's not perfect and Mom and you get mad at him, but I still love him. It would be easier for me if you didn't talk about him in front of me."

Stepfathers Feel Guilty

Stepfathers who have children of their own have a lot of guilt. Men in this country are taught that to be successful they must make lots of money and take good care of their families. So when a marriage is so bad that the husband separates from his wife, he feels like a failure on several counts: he has not only left his wife, but he has also left his kids, and he feels even more guilty about that because they didn't do anything wrong. In fact, people often stay together much longer than they should just because of their kids. Some people just don't think much of a man who leaves his family (even if his wife wanted him to leave). This is exactly what happened to David. He and his wife, Joan, divorced after eleven years of marriage, and

David left his three sons, who were eight, five, and two years old. He loved his boys a lot and it was hard to leave them. Then David met Carol, who had three little boys eight, six, and five. When David and Carol were first married and his boys came to visit them on weekends, David would get real weird and withdraw from everyone.

One time Carol told him that she thought his boys needed more affection from him when they came over, and he said, "Well, I can't give everybody the same amount of affection, so I thought it would be better if I didn't give any. Then no one will get jealous." He felt he only had so much love, so there wouldn't be enough for everyone.

Well, as you might guess, David's boys felt very jealous anyway, because here he was living with these three stepsons and going to Boy Scouts and Little League with them. Since he wasn't giving his own sons any affection, they figured he loved those new boys more. Carol and David were able to talk about it and decided that all the boys needed him in different ways. His own kids were used to more affection from him and needed that, as well as some private time with him.

David is pretty comfortable showing lots of interest in his stepsons when his kids aren't around. But every now and then when he talks to his boys on the phone, or gets a letter (his sons moved to a different part of the country a few years ago), he still feels guilty about the time he spends with his stepsons, instead of his own sons. Then he withdraws from his stepsons a little bit, or gets really angry with them about something they did or didn't do.

Guilt is something that never goes away entirely, but it sure helps to talk about it. It might also help you to understand that when your stepdad has cycles of interest and uninterest in you, or acts weird when his real kids are around, part of his problem may be that he is feeling guilty.

Stepfathers Feel Like They Have to Be "Superdads" to Their Own Kids

Because of the guilt that stepfathers have, some of them feel they have to show their own kids a spectacular time when they see them. So if a father goes to see his children on the weekends, he probably plans trips to amusement parks, skiing, camping, and other pretty exciting activities to prove to himself and his kids that he is still a good father. If you see your stepfather only at dinner every night and watch him work around the house on the weekend, you might feel resentful when you hear about the wonderful things he does with his own kids. Maybe you feel the only time your family does anything fun is when your stepdad's kids come to visit, which seems unfair to you. It might help you to understand that your stepdad is doing a lot of this out of guilt, and that after a "fun-packed" weekend, he is probably exhausted.

Stepfathers Feel Like a Walking Wallet

If your stepdad was married before and has children, he probably pays child support for them every month, and maybe alimony to his ex-wife as well. Now he has to contribute money to his new family too, and it seems to him that there never is enough money. He feels like he can't win because whoever he spends money on, his first family or his stepfamily, the other group usually feels cheated—or he feels they do. No one is satisfied, and the pressure to provide for everyone grows.

Your stepdad feels that his efforts to work real hard and provide for you is a way of showing love, and he assumes that you will see this and feel grateful. Because this is a very indirect way of showing love, it may not feel at all like he cares for you. But many stepdads have said to us,

"Of course I care about my stepkids. Why do you think I work my tail off twelve hours a day?" Kids usually take that role for granted, and we don't know any kid who feels loved because his parent makes a lot of money. But ineffective as it is, earning money is the only way some stepfathers know to show their love.

9 ∗ How to Live with Your Kind of Stepfather

The Dictator (and how he got that way)

Many men who are in their thirties and forties had dads who were heavily into discipline. These dads felt it was their responsibility to accomplish two things with their sons: make sure they were responsible about chores, school, and work, and make sure that they learned to follow orders. Other issues, such as having a warm relationship and good communication, were not seen as very important. Since most people tend to treat their children as they were treated by their parents, there is now another generation of men who value the same things: responsibility and making sure their kids behave. This is how they define being a good father.

When these thirty- and forty-year-old men become stepfathers, they naturally approach their stepkids with a heavy hand. After the divorce, your mom was probably busy working and putting her own life back together, so your behavior may have been a bit unruly. Your mother may have said, "I need your help with the kids," and the stepfather responds in the way that's natural to him. He comes on like Hitler. The minute one of these men becomes a stepfather, he feels it's his duty to shape up his stepkids.

One stepfather I know said, "The first time I met my wife's kids, one of them was standing on the back of the sofa, and when I turned my back, he leaped on me. I felt like I was walking into a zoo, every time I went over there. They were so wild it was clear she needed my help with them."

These stepkids, of course, hated this stranger coming in and telling them what to do. The teenage boy in effect said, "No way, José," and the war was on. No self-respecting teenager is going to be bossed around by someone he or she doesn't know and respect. Mom's caught in the middle. She wants help, but when her new husband gets tough, she usually resents him for it, and winds up defending her kids. The stepfather gets angry and feels like a failure with his new family.

These stepfathers are in trouble on two counts. First, all stepfathers need to become friends with their stepchildren before they begin parenting. Second, as mentioned above, teenagers don't like being told what to do. Since no one involved knows much about parenting, much less stepparenting, this kind of stepfather is doomed to failure with his stepkids. He and the whole family are victims of his training.

How to Cope

Talk to your stepfather and try to explain how you feel. Try to stay calm when he is bossing you around, since, if you get angry and yell back at him, he will probably get more angry and more unreasonable. Instead, present your side of things when you're not furious and see if he will negotiate.

Show your dad the list of "friending" behaviors in Appendix II, "Friending."

How Not to Say It

"Will you get off my back!"

"Who the hell do you think you are, telling me what to do! You're not my real father."

"Geez, did you take lessons from Hitler?"

How to Say It

"It feels like you're only interested in ordering me around and trying to change me. I think we'd get along much better if we could discuss what you want me to do."

"I know you feel real concerned that I'm going to grow up a mess. But I think I could learn a lot more from you if you would discuss things with me, rather than order me around."

Mr. Grouch

This stepfather is always upset with what you do or don't do, but, unlike Hitler, he doesn't let you know directly. Instead he just walks around looking grumpy, mumbling to himself, giving you dirty looks, or telling your mother how irresponsible and lazy you are. Occasionally he may blow up or shout an order, but most of the time you may just have a vague feeling that he doesn't like you.

Mr. Grouch often says he did like his stepkids a lot in the beginning, but his expectations of their behavior got in the way of developing a better relationship with them. He expects kids, especially teenagers, to be responsible, polite, helpful, and obedient. He either has had little experience with teenagers, or he forgets what it felt like to one himself—or both. As he becomes more and more disappointed with his stepkids' behavior, he gets grouchier and grouchier. He thinks kids should keep their rooms picked up and do their chores without being reminded. He can't understand why they don't care about how the house or kitchen looks, and in general sees them as being selfish, inconsiderate, rude, and generally "bad."

The problem with Mr. Grouch is that he isn't able to talk about his feelings very well. When he does talk, it's always to his wife about how bad her kids are. Why doesn't she do something?! The only way he knows how to express his disappointment and anger to his stepkids is to act grouchy, and his stepkids don't know what they are doing to make him dislike them so much.

Hank was a perfect Mr. Grouch. He married Jill when her children were four and seven. The family got along pretty well until Kari, the oldest child, turned twelve or thirteen. Kari was very social and very popular, and as soon as she started high school she wanted a lot of new freedom. When her parents restricted her, she became quite rebellious toward them and began acting real snotty. As the situation escalated, Hank got grouchier and grouchier and did not speak at all to Kari except to bark an order now and then. Kari began swearing at her parents and running away to a friend's house when things got too hot at home. Hank could not accept any of this behavior and could not talk with Kari about it. He decided that Kari was "bad" and he could not see how his grouchy behavior contributed to her feeling "bad" and acting "bad."

To make things more complicated, Hank had two older teenagers from his first marriage. They lived in a nearby town, and they would visit quite often as they were growing up. In fact the only time Hank wasn't grouchy was when his own kids were visiting. Hank, of course, loved his own kids dearly and thought they were wonderful. He never saw them behave in any of the ways that Kari was behaving. (They probably only acted like that at home with their mother and their own stepfather.) So Hank thought he knew about teenagers and he couldn't accept that Kari's behavior was normal. Hank's solution was for Kari to "change" her behavior. Kari was too old to become a sweet, compliant child again—her biological clock had moved past that time—but neither was she mature enough to have very good control over her anger and frustration at home.

Hank's solution to the problem was to become more withdrawn at home and not speak to Kari at all. This was not a very happy solution, especially since both Hank and Kari wanted to like each other. This family may have to go into a holding pattern for a few years until Kari matures a little more, gets better control of her anger, and has a little more freedom to be away from home. Then perhaps she and Hank can get things worked out between them.

How to Cope

Remind yourself that people act grouchy when they feel disappointed, hurt, and angry and they don't know how to express those feelings. When you're feeling brave, you may want to open up conversations with your stepdad that would allow him to level with you. Pick a calm moment and open with, "You really get upset when . . ." or "It really bothers you when I . . ."

You may also want to try to let your stepdad know how his grouchiness makes you feel. "When you act grouchy, I feel afraid of you," or "I feel like I can't do anything to please you. No matter what I do, it feels like you hate me."

You might also work on trying to get your stepdad involved in friendly conversation. Ask his opinion on something, ask him to help you with something, or ask him to come to your game or an event at school. Sometimes grouchiness is a habit and it takes practicing other kinds of conversation to get rid of it.

The Cold and Indifferent Stepfather

Dick Conners was a perfect example of this type. He is a real macho guy who is immature and self-centered. He likes his wife, their sex life, and his cars. That's all he makes time for and he has no interest whatsoever in his stepchildren. He thinks of them as his wife's children and says flat out that they are her responsibility and her problem. When his children from a previous marriage come to visit, he will include his stepkids in family outings, but that's the extent of his contact with them. Some teenagers are perfectly happy with this arrangement. They keep busy and out of the house and don't worry about their stepdad too much. They simply don't expect anything of him. Other kids take it very personally if someone doesn't seem to care about them. They may knock themselves out trying to please their stepfather or to get some kind of interest from him, positive or negative.

How to Cope

Tell your stepdad you'd like to spend more time with him. He may not be at all interested, but it won't hurt to ask.

Don't feel that there must be something wrong with you because your stepdad is so cold. He's got the problem. He may be so self-centered that he never even thinks about you, good or bad. Or it may be that he's very guilty about not being with his own kids and ignores you so he won't feel even more guilty.

Try to expect nothing from your stepfather so you won't be disappointed all the time.

If you've tried to be nice to your stepdad and it doesn't do any good, then put your energy into other relationships with your mom, real dad, other adults, and friends who can give you more signs of caring.

Mr. Hot Pants

This type of stepfather comes on in a very sexy way with his stepdaughter. Sometimes he "accidentally" brushes against her breasts. At other times he may give her long good-night kisses. This sexy behavior is subtle, but you get the message and are very uncomfortable around him. Other stepfathers in this category are right out front with their sexual advances, crawl in bed with their stepdaughters or talk with them about going to bed together. We will talk more about sexy stepfathers in Chapter 13, "Sex in Your Stepfamily." This is a very serious situation, and if you don't do anything about it, it will only get worse. Your stepdad is probably not going to stop what he's doing, so unfortunately, it's really up to you to protect yourself.

How to Cope

If you think your stepfather is acting sexy, you're probably right. Don't try to talk yourself out of it by thinking maybe you're too sensitive or imagining things. Make sure *you* are not behaving in a provocative way, like parading around the house in a towel, underwear, or a sheer nightie, or initiating a lot of snuggling with your stepfather.

Tell your stepfather in no uncertain terms to stop what he's doing. For example, "Stop brushing against me," or "I don't want to kiss you anymore."

Talk to your mother. Tell her what is happening. I know it's hard to tell your mom and you don't want to ruin her marriage, but she needs to know, even if it's painful for her to hear. It's a good idea to tell your mother that you are very frightened and need to tell someone if she can't help you herself.

Sometimes mothers cannot handle the information, so they react by not believing you. If this happens, you must tell another responsible adult: a teacher to whom you feel close, a school counselor, your minister, or another adult.

If you just can't bring yourself to tell anyone, then see if you can arrange to live with someone else—your real dad, a friend, or another relative. If the situation is very bad, you may even want to try a foster home.

How to Say It (to Stepdad)

"If you don't stop kissing me like that/brushing against me, I'm going to tell Mom and if Mom doesn't do anything, I plan to talk to my school counselor."

How to Say It (to Mom)

"It's hard for me to tell you this, Mom, because I don't want you to be unhappy, but I feel scared about the way Bill tries to kiss me, and the way he brushes against my body. I told him to stop and he did for a while, but now it's starting to happen again."

The Invisible Stepfather

If your mother was divorced and the head of your household for a long time, five years or more, she may not want to give up being in charge. So when she remarries, it is not because she needs someone to help her with the kids and other responsibilities, it is because she wants a husband and companion. If this is the case, your stepfather may move into your house, but not take much of a parenting role at all with you.

You may find that pleasant, but still worry that he doesn't like you or is not really interested in you. You may also feel jealous of his exclusive relationship with your mom. In these situations, the family may not be as close as other stepfamilies, but that is okay. This style of marriage is very appropriate. Your stepfather's main job in this case is to be your mother's friend and companion. It is hard not to feel left out or rejected, but you would probably hate it if he really took over as the head of the household, and started telling you what to do. If you would like more of a relationship with him, then you should let him know clearly that it's okay with you if he gets more involved in your life. For example, you could invite him to a school play or football game.

The Stepfather Who Has No Children of His Own

If your stepfather has no children from a previous marriage, in some ways he will have an easier time fitting into your family. First of all, he has no guilt about the children he has left, as a lot of stepfathers do. Secondly, he does not know the special love feelings a parent has for his own children, so he doesn't measure his feelings for you on that yardstick. He also doesn't think that he should love you like he would love his own kids. In a way, he is free to like you, or love you, and to let it come naturally.

On the other hand, this stepfather may have more difficulty figuring out what to do about discipline than a more experienced father, and it will take him longer to understand you because he hasn't been around kids. He will probably have unrealistic expectations of you and feel angry because you aren't the way he thinks you should be. (These stepdads can also be very touchy about their possessions.)

Mary Ann and her three children moved into Tom's four-bedroom home. Tom had worked hard at his sales job to be able to afford his home and he was very proud of it. He lived alone in his house for several years before he and Mary Ann married, and Tom was a confirmed neatnick. Everything was spotless, and he had a lot of rules about how things should be. The garden hose had to be wound up in a tight little circle, the magazines arranged in a special order on the coffee table, and so on.

As you can imagine, when Mary Ann and her kids

moved in, all hell broke loose. Tom could not adjust to his stepkids "messing up *his* house," and the kids hated living there. Even after several months of counseling, Tom and Mary Ann decided to split up. Tom just couldn't adjust to sharing his home and possessions with children.

How to Cope

Tell your stepdad you are having a hard time measuring up to what he expects of you. Let him know that you feel put down and criticized a lot of the time.

Be specific about the areas where you think he is expecting too much.

Do not touch or borrow your stepdad's personal possessions without asking.

Encourage your stepfather to go to activities in which you are involved. There he will have a chance to see other kids your age in action and talk to other parents.

How Not To Say It

(Sarcastically) "I'm sure I never do a thing right, according to you."

"It's a good thing you never had any kids of your own. They'd be a mess!"

How To Say It

"I want you to know that I really do try to do a good job on the yard, but it never seems to be what you want. Can we talk about what exactly you want done, and I'll be honest about whether or not I can accomplish that?"

"I'm having a hard time being the kind of kid you want me to be. Can we talk about it?"

Physically Abusive Stepfathers

We've met very few stepfathers who beat their stepchildren, but there are some who do. If your stepfather hits or beats you, then it is a very serious problem. There are lots of reasons why people beat their stepchildren but no excuses. Often, the beatings happen when the person has been drinking a lot and has lost control of himself. Some stepfathers batter their kids because they are very frustrated and angry at other people in their lives, and take it out on you because you are a handy target. Still other stepfathers are abusive because that's the way they were brought up. Their father or mother beat on them and they do the same thing to you because that's the way they were taught to handle anger.

If you have this kind of stepfather, then you've got a problem with your mom, too, because she is not protecting you very well. It is her job to make sure that you are not harmed. Unfortunately, we have found that when a man is beating up his children, he is often beating his wife as well. The mothers are not able to protect either themselves or their children, and everyone is in jeopardy.

How to Cope

If your mother is not aware your stepfather is beating you, then you must tell her so she can take steps to protect you.

If your mother *is* aware your stepfather is hitting you and is unable or unwilling to stop him, then you need to get help outside your family.

Tell someone who can help about the beatings, such as your family doctor, minister, school counselor, or teacher, or go to the police station and talk to an officer. Child abuse is against the law, and doctors and counselors are required by law in most states to report to the police what is happening and get help for you.

You may feel a little guilty "telling" on your stepfather, but you are doing both him and yourself a favor by doing so. He probably feels guilty about what he's doing, and he will benefit if he is made to stop and learn other ways to handle his feelings.

If you are not comfortable with any of the above suggestions, you may want to explore the possibility of finding another place to live, without telling anyone other than your mother the real reason.

The Stepfather Who Is Caring and Reasonable

This kind of stepfather has pretty good communication with you, is interested in your activities, and spends time with you. He leaves most of the discipline up to your mom until you and he are fairly good friends and he feels accepted and respected by you. When he has to discipline, he is most often fair. He is the kind of guy who likes kids and usually enjoys playing himself, so it's easy to make friends with him. He doesn't push you to be close, and he lets you set the pace and make many of the rules in the relationship. Lucky you!

10 * Visiting Mom, Visiting Dad

When your parents live in two different homes, life can be complicated. Sometimes it's great; other times it's awful. In this chapter we'll be discussing what it's like to go back and forth: the advantages, some of the problems, and how you can feel more comfortable with your particular situation.

Visitation

In most divorces one of your parents gets legal custody of you and the other has visitation rights. This means that when your parents were divorced it was decided, either by your parents or by the courts, that you should live with one parent (usually your mother) and that that parent has the legal power to make all the decisions about your life. The other parent was allowed to visit you or to have you visit him or her on a regular basis.

Today, the courts in many states are moving toward the idea of joint legal custody, which means that both parents have equal say in how you should be raised. They have also tried to work out more equal living arrangements so that children can spend more time with the "absent" parent. This certainly makes more sense, doesn't it? Some children even live equally with two parents.

Jody's mom and dad live in the same general neighbor-hood, and Jody spends four days with her mom and then the next day she goes home from school on a different bus and spends three days at her dad's house. She has clothes, toys, and everything she needs at each house, and so she only carries a small Teddy Bear in her backpack on the days that she switches.

Some children spend one week at Mom's and one week at Dad's. Other kids spend the school year at Mom's and some holidays and most of the summer at Dad's. Since you are a little older, you probably live with one parent and visit the other on weekends or vacations.

Feeling Like an Outsider

The main problem with visiting the parent you don't live with, especially if she or he is remarried and has stepkids living there, is that you feel like a visitor! That's a crummy way to feel with your very own dad or mom. For example, your dad may expect you to fit right in, and to amuse your-self with your stepbrothers or stepsisters, because he may feel unsure about giving you any extra attention. He is try-ing to get along with his stepchildren, and may feel like he's in a bind about how much attention to give everyone. Then you may feel like you have lost your dad to his new wife and her kids. Ugh!

If this other family does things differently, it may be real hard for you to accept that their way is okay. Maybe your stepparent makes hamburger patties flat instead of fat, or the only snack they buy is yogurt, or they buy the "wrong" kind of cereal. You may find yourself making all kinds of judgments about the food they eat, the way it's cooked, the kind of furniture they have, the kind of Christ-mas tree they buy, or how they decorate it. You are used to your family's way of doing things and probably feel that your mom or dad is betraying you by going along with all these new weird ways. They may seem dumb to you, and

[81]

it's hard to get used to these strange ways and strange rules.

How to Cope

Explain to your dad or mom that you are feeling like an outsider. Ask him or her to spend some special time alone with you each time you visit.

Tell your mom or dad that it would help you if you had a special place of your own in their house. It isn't always possible for you to have your own room, of course, but most kids feel more at home if they have a private shelf in a closet, or a drawer where they can leave things from visit to visit.

Express your willingness to take on certain responsibilities when you are visiting. Maybe there are a couple of jobs that you could do each time you are there. You will feel more a part of the family, and if your stepparent has kids, they won't resent you as much if you pitch in with the work.

Expect to follow the rules of the house you are in. Your mom or dad and stepmom or stepdad really don't want to hear about what time you have to come in at home, or that your parent at home doesn't care if you leave your shoes in the living room. You will feel like more a part of that family if you try to follow their rules and accept their ways and they will appreciate you for trying to fit in. You will also benefit by learning more about different ways to live than you would if you had only one family.

If you are asked what kind of vegetable you like, or what kind of cereal you like, don't be shy about saying. On the other hand, try not to be real critical about their choices, either. You might volunteer to go to the store with your parent or stepparent to help with the shopping. If you did this, there is a pretty good chance you would be asked for your opinion. Even if you hate the food, you

[82]

probably will not starve to death during the few days or few weeks you are visiting.

How Not to Say It

"All you care about are these kids and Shirley. Why should I come over here?"

"I don't have to go to bed at eleven at home. My mom lets me stay up as late as I want. I'm not a baby, you know."

How to Say It

"Dad, I'm having a hard time feeling like I belong here. I feel real left out of this family. Could you and I spend some time alone together when I come? I come to see you and I think it would feel better to me if *you* could just take me out sometimes without the rest of the family."

"It's hard for me to follow these new rules when I'm here. Can we talk about all of the rules you expect me to follow? I feel like I don't know what's going on until I break one and then everyone gets mad at me."

Stepfamily "Jet Lag"

You may find that it is hard on you emotionally when it's time to leave your mom's and go to your dad's or vice versa. Some kids become a little withdrawn, others irritable or a little hyper right before they have to leave one house and right after they arrive at the other. One of your parents may blame the other parent because you feel upset and act weird, but it's just your way of making a difficult adjustment. Any kind of change is stressful, and we all react to stress in different ways. You might think of it as a kind of "jet lag."

How to Cope

Give yourself time to think and plan for each move back and forth. Try to figure out what helps you adjust the best. Maybe you need a little time by yourself in your room or in a private place for a little while before you leave one home and after you arrive at the other.

Maybe it helps you to have some time to talk privately with your mom or dad right before you leave or right after you arrive.

Explain to your parents that you may be a little hard to get along with when you first get home because it's difficult going back and forth.

Feeling That You Don't Have Control Over Your Life

Rosalind, age seventeen, was jubilant this past Christmas. For the first time in the fifteen years her parents had been divorced she was able to spend Christmas the way *she* wanted. She said, "Finally I don't have to go anywhere for Christmas. I can spend the whole time in one place." Lots of kids have the same feelings of powerlessness. While they want to see their absent parent, they hate having to stick to a schedule of visitation that has nothing to do with what is going on in their lives. For example, friends are extremely important to you, as they should be, and you would like to spend a lot of time with them. But you are obligated to spend some time with your absent parent. A solution might be to negotiate with that parent to find times that would work best for both of you.

Let's say it's your weekend to visit Dad but your best friend is having a huge slumber party you don't want to miss, or your girlfriend is really putting the heat on you to take her out. What do you do? While it would be tempting to talk to your mom and see if she can get your visit changed for you, that's not the best idea in the long run. One of the important tasks for you as a teenager is to learn to deal with both parents directly, and to negotiate with them. Besides, the chances are pretty good that your dad might feel suspicious of your mother's motives if she asks and they might end up in a fight. It would be much better if you approach your absent parent and explain that there's something you really want to do this weekend that conflicts with your going to see her or him. Ask if it would be okay if you did not come Friday night but came on Saturday night or Sunday instead. Another option is to use your absent parent's home as a base camp for the weekend (if it is fairly close to where you live). The way this works is that you do in fact live at Dad's or Mom's for the weekend but still get to go to some of your own activities anyway. This is a compromise that works well for both you and your parent. Your parent still gets to see you on and off during the weekend and you are able to do some of the things you want with your friends.

How Not to Say It

Call up Dad Friday afternoon and say, "Dad, I've got the flu. I'm not going to be able to come this weekend."

"Mom says she wants me to stay home this weekend so I can't come over."

How to Say It

"Dad, I would like to see you this weekend, but there's a school dance Saturday night that I really want to go to. Would it be okay if I spend all day Sunday and Sunday evening with you instead?"

Feeling Disloyal and Guilty

Sue lives with her mother in a small apartment. Sue's mother is a salesperson in a pet store and her salary is not large, so money is tight. Sue's mom is still pretty broken up about her divorce, doesn't date at all, and lives a very quiet life. Sue's dad's life is quite different. He remarried a woman who is a vice-president of an electronics company and since there are two incomes, they have plenty of money. They have a large house with a pool.

When Sue goes to see her father and stepmother she's torn by a lot of feelings. She loves seeing her father, really likes her stepmother, and enjoys the fun things they do together, such as eating out a lot, skiing, and going to the movies. **But at the same time, Sue feels disloyal to her own mother since she likes her stepmother so much. She also feels guilty that she enjoys her father's money while her mother has so little, and when she's with her dad, she worries about her mother sitting at home all alone. Because of all her mixed feelings, Sue says that sometimes she is bitchy to her stepmother, which makes her feel even more guilty!**

How to Cope

Remind yourself periodically that your parents are responsible for their decision to divorce, not you. As a matter of fact, if you had your own way, your parents would probably still be married. It's also important to remember that you did not cause your parents' divorce. Even if you were hell on wheels as a kid and your parents argued about what to do with you, you were not the cause of their marriage ending. The problem was that your parents didn't know how to talk to one another and solve problems together. They most likely fought or disagreed about a lot of things besides you: money, sex, jobs, etc.

Since you are not responsible for your parents' divorce, you certainly are not responsible for what's happening in their lives now. If one of your parents is sad and lonely it is that person's task to work through these feelings and find a more satisfactory life. If you like a steppar-ent, that does not mean that you like your own parent any less. You've simply found a new friend, and that's okay. If your mother or father is sending you messages that you really shouldn't like your new stepmother or stepfather, try to put that message in perspective. Your parent is inse-cure and jealous, and while those feelings are painful for your parent, they remain your parent's problem to solve. *You* can't do anything about those feelings! Any warm feelings you have for your stepparent are okay.

When the Grass Looks Greener on the Other Side

After his mom and dad were divorced, Joel lived with his mom and only visited with his dad and his dad's new fam-ily. Joel and his mom had a real hard time getting along to-gether. Joel was pretty rebellious, did not do very well in school, and had a terrible temper. He would get furious at his mom and yell that he wished he could live with his dad. He loved going to his dad's. No one bugged him there. His stepmother was very nice to him and spent a lot of time lis-tening to Joel and helping him with his problems. Joel's stepmom had two teenage boys a little older than Joel, and they were usually doing something fun when Joel was there.

One day Joel got so mad he kicked a door in, and his mom decided she just couldn't handle it anymore. She made arrangements with Joel's dad and stepmom for him to live with them. Joel was extremely happy . . . for about a month. Then reality set in. Joel discovered that during the week there were many jobs and responsibilites to be taken care of at his new home. His stepmom worked, and the boys had to do a lot of the housework. Joel wasn't used to doing much at home, and this was very hard on him. He also discovered that his dad and stepmom had very high standards for those jobs, for getting schoolwork done, and for his behavior in general. Joel had a very hard time living up to those expectations and usually felt like a failure. He had had no idea it would be this way!

While he had a lot of freedom at his mom's, his dad expected him to be home more and always wanted to know where he was. Joel also missed his buddies. He had a hard time making new friends, and his stepbrothers were not quite as nice to him as they had been on the weekend visits. In fact, they resented Joel's being there, and resented his not wanting to do his share of the work. It wasn't too long before Joel was begging to move back to his mom's. All the adults decided that his dad's house was a much better place for him to be and that even though he was miserable, he would have to learn to adjust and to cope with the new home.

His dad and stepmom went to counseling with Joel, and they all did a lot of work to help Joel become happier and to adjust to the new behavior expected of him. So, while this situation was probably best for Joel in the long run, he was not very happy about it, and he was sorry he had moved.

Sometimes, teenagers want to live with the other parent just to be away from a parent they are having difficulty getting along with. They often don't know what they are getting into, because visiting on weekends does not give you a very realistic picture of what living with your other parent would be like. Most of your problems go with you, and you may even have some new ones that you never thought of.

When Your Parents Use You as a Messenger

If your parents are still mad at each other or uncomfortable talking to one another, they may use you to carry messages back and forth. "Tell your father to send the support check on time next month!" or, "Tell your mother I'll be picking you up early next week." Delivering these messages puts you in an awful position because your mother or father may not like what they're hearing and may get mad at you. "What the hell does she mean about the support, I pay it on time every month!" Suddenly you're stuck explaining what she or he meant.

Your situation is a little like that of messengers in ancient times. If a messenger delivered a message to a king and the king didn't like the message, he would take out his anger on the messenger by having him beheaded!

How to Cope

Since there's no way your parents are going to fire you as messenger, you're going to have to quit, and this will take some courage on your part. The way to do this is to tell both your parents that you can no longer deliver messages for either of them and would they please give their messages to each other, instead of through you.

This would be a good time to talk to both of your parents about making your own arrangements for visiting rather than having them in control of that.

How to Say It

"Mom, every time I give Dad one of your messages he gets upset. And when I give you his messages, you get mad, too. When you guys get mad, I feel miserable. So I've decided not to deliver messages for either of you anymore."

When You Don't Want to Visit as Often

"I really love my dad and like seeing him and everything, but I want to be with my friends more," says Jamie. "Nobody wants me for a friend if I'm never here on the weekend. Besides, it's getting real boring at Dad's. I don't like just following him around and watching him work all weekend any more. It's either that or watch TV. Big deal."

Jamie is twelve now and has been visiting her dad every weekend for the past three years. Her problem is how to tell her dad. This is probably one of the hardest things she'll ever have to say to anyone in her whole life.

How to Cope

First of all, talk about your feelings with the parent that you live with so she or he knows how you feel and what you want. If your divorced parents have a pretty good relationship, that parent may be able to help you out by talking about your feelings with your other parent and working it out so you can spend more time with your friends.

If your parents don't get along well, it will not work to have them discuss the problem. It will be better if you tell your absent parent yourself. As you get older, it is better for you to work out your own schedule and make your own arrangements with your absent parent, anyway.

Remember that it is absolutely normal and okay for you to want to spend more time with your friends and less time with either parent! It's impossible to pull away like this without hurting your parents' feelings a little bit. It always hurts every parent a little when their kids don't want to spend as much time with them as they used to. But they will get over their hurt and disappointment.

How Not to Say It

"It's so boring over here. I don't see why I have to come every weekend."

How to Say It

"Mom (or Dad), I love you a lot and like getting to see you on the weekends but I've got a problem. I also want to spend more time with my friends. Would it be okay with you if I saw you every other weekend instead of every weekend?"

Another alternative is to ask if you can bring a friend along sometimes.

If Your Parents Still Don't Understand

Parents have a hard time letting go of growing kids, and even if you explain nicely what you want, they just may not understand. If your absent parent says, "No way. You have to come every weekend!" then you need legal help. The parent you live with can go to court and ask the judge to change the ruling about how often you see your absent parent. The judge will probably want to talk to you and will be very interested in what you want. Don't be too afraid of the judge. He or she is just a regular person who has a job dealing with law. And a judge will be more concerned with what's best for you than with what either your mother or your father wants. Most judges are very interested in seeing that kids are happy.

The Advantages of Having Two Homes

One fifteen-year-old boy we know talked about visiting his dad's house every other weekend. ''I really like going to my dad's house. My mother is always on my case about something: my hair, my room, feeding the dogs, something! At my dad's they're just glad to see me and I can relax.'' Both he and his mother, then, get a break from each other and feel glad to see each other when he returns on Sunday night.

Other kids mention that the parent they're visiting really pays attention to them, listens more closely to what they have to say, and doesn't seem distracted.

One of the big advantages for you in having two households to live in is that you get to see first hand the different ways people can relate to each other. Debbie has lived with her father and stepmother since she was eight and has visited her mother and her mother's live-in boyfriend every other weekend for the past five years. ''My father and stepmother have a real close relationship. They talk a lot, both sing in the choir at church and hardly do anything apart. My mother and Dave [her live-in] are just the opposite. They're both independent and like to do their own thing. I'm a lot like my mother so I'll probably want my marriage to be more like hers, but there's some things I like about my dad's situation, too. Who knows! Maybe I can have it all!

And, let's face it. Kids whose parents have divorced usually get lots more goodies. You probably have at least two Christmases, celebrate your birthday twice, and sometimes get to go on vacations with both of your families.

(92)

11 * When You Don't See One of Your Parents

There are a number of kids who never see one of their parents. This happens in several ways: sometimes a parent disappears out of your life after your parents divorce, or sometimes he or she gradually just sees you less and less. In other cases the parent you live with doesn't think your other parent is good for you and has done lots of things to prevent your absent parent from seeing you. Some of you have lost one of your parents through death or a totally debilitating mental or physical illness. If you are one of those people who never sees one of your parents, you have experienced an enormous loss in your life. Nothing is more devastating than to lose a natural parent. You need tremendous amounts of love from your parents, and when one is gone, you don't even know if that parent loved you or not. Even people who are adopted often become very curious about their natural parents, and sometimes even begin searching for them. One of the things they need to find out is if that parent loved them. In this chapter we will discuss some of these situations.

One Parent Says You Can't See Your Other Parent

Chris, fifteen, hasn't seen his dad for four years. He lives with his mom, who is so hurt and angry about her divorce that she is getting back at her ex-husband by not letting him see Chris. Vicki, a senior in high school, has seen her mother only once in the last two years for a very different reason. Vicki's father doesn't think Vicki's mother is a good example for Vicki because her mother has a different boyfriend living at her home just about every week. In both cases the parents' divorce papers say Chris and Vicki can have "reasonable visitation" with their absent parent. Both Chris and Vicki would like to see their absent parents a lot more than they do now, but they don't know how.

How to Cope

Talk to the parent you live with and tell him or her that you would like to see your mother or father more than you do. You might want to say something like "I know Mom's not perfect, but she is my mom and I'd really like to see her."

See if you can get a friend, minister, or school counselor to talk to your parent about allowing you more visitation with your absent parent.

If the parent you live with still refuses, then let them know you've decided to get in touch with your absent parent yourself. This way your parent knows what you plan to do and you are not being sneaky.

Call your absent parent and say you would really like to see him or her more than you are. This will take a lot of courage, especially if you are not sure whether that parent loves you or not. A couple of things might happen.

It is unlikely, but your parent might be rather cold. What's more likely is that your parent may have been feeling rejected and will appreciate your taking the first step. If your parent seems receptive, you may decide to ask him or her to do what is necessary legally to make sure you get to see one another more often.

If there is no legal reason you can't see your absent parent, then make plans to do so. You could meet your mother or father after school once a week, visit her or him on Saturday or meet at a park. It's best to tell the parent you live with what you are doing to avoid worry about where you are.

Why Your Absent Parent Never Comes to See You

If your parent hasn't come to see you in a real long time, you may feel very hurt, angry, puzzled, or rejected. Most kids in this situation decide that something must be really wrong with them; they think they've been bad in some way or are unlovable. These are very painful feelings for you to carry around day after day, so it's real important that you look at other reasons why your parent doesn't seem to be interested in seeing you.

It's Too Painful to See You

Some men and women are so hurt by their divorce that they cannot bring themselves ever to lay eyes on their former mate again. In order to avoid this, your absent parent gives up seeing you in the process. Your parent may really want to see you but thinks that means having to see your other parent as well, and is afraid he or she will fall apart if that happens. This kind of thinking sounds a little strange, but it's not unusual in divorced people.

[95]

Your Parent Feels Rejected by You

A man we know, Don, loves his two children a lot but no longer sees them. When we asked him why he told us the following story: His ex-wife Louise was so angry at him for divorcing her that she decided to turn the kids against him. Louise would tell the kids that their dad didn't really love them, that he was only coming to see them out of duty, and that they would have a lousy time when they went to his house. She also told the kids all the gory details of their marriage, making Don the bad guy in every situation.

After a year of this continual brainwashing, the kids grew more and more hostile to their father. When he went to pick them up, they would pout and not talk and everyone would have a miserable time. Then Louise started telling Don that the kids couldn't see him because they were sick or had other plans. After a couple of years Don gave up trying to see his kids, because they made it clear they didn't want to see him. When he talked about this, he was quite sad.

Your Parent Doesn't Want to Confuse You

George and Jane were divorced when their little boy, Alan, was two years old. Soon after the divorce, Jane remarried, so Alan had a new stepfather. George decided that he didn't want Alan torn apart year after year visiting between two homes, having two fathers, and so on. Even though it was hard on George, he stopped seeing his son so his son could have a better life.

We happen to think that George is wrong in the decision he made. As most of you know, visiting between two homes and having two fathers is better than losing your real father entirely, and most kids adjust to stepfamily life pretty well. Alan will never know his real father, and as he gets older, he can't help but assume that he wasn't lovable enough or his real father would still be around. Kids need love from as many adults as possible, and especially need to know that their real parents loved them.

Your Parent Is Self-Centered

There are a very small number of parents who just plain don't care about their kids. When they get divorced, they're not that interested in seeing their kids anymore. These parents have not grown up and are not able to think of anyone but themselves. Maybe they didn't get enough love from their own parents. In any case, they are not capable of loving a child because they just don't have any extra love to give. They find parenting too demanding and they simply can't handle it.

Shawn's dad was like this. He disappeared after the divorce, stopped paying Shawn's child support, didn't work very much, and what money he did earn he spent on drugs. Every few years, if he was in town, he would call Shawn and come to see him. He made Shawn all kinds of promises about the future and all kinds of excuses about the past. Shawn needed so badly for his father to love him that he made up excuses for his father, too. "He has been real busy working," Shawn would say.

He would often blame his mother for not letting his dad see him. When Shawn was about thirteen, he began to think in more grown-up ways and he started to face the fact that his father was irresponsible and never would really love Shawn as Shawn had hoped. This was very difficult for Shawn to accept, and he and his mom went to a counselor to get help in facing the truth. Now Shawn says, "I know my dad loves me in his own way, as much as he is able to love anybody, which is not very much. I think after I grow up I will probably try to spend some time with him and try to understand him better, but I don't kid myself anymore. If I want to see my dad, I am going to have to go to him because he just can't get it together enough to come to me. Maybe someday he'll grow up."

If Your Mom or Dad Is Mentally Ill or Alcoholic

Having a natural parent who is mentally ill or who is an alcoholic is something like having a self-centered parent, except that your mom or dad can't be an adequate parent to you because of illness. You may feel unloved, angry, or even full of hate; those feelings are entirely normal. But you still may feel very guilty for having those feelings because you've been told that your mom or dad is sick and can't help his or her problem. Maybe you even took care of that parent before the divorce and now you feel guilty for leaving, or for not taking care of him or her anymore.

Sabrina's mom suffers from a chronic mental illness. She was in the hospital a lot of the time before the divorce. When she was home, though, Sabrina took care of her as well as doing most of the housework and cooking. When Sabrina's parents were divorced, Sabrina went to live with her dad, and her mom had to go back into the hospital for a while. Sabrina felt like she abandoned her mom and still feels guilty about that. Her mother lives in an apartment in another city now, and Sabrina goes to see her sometimes. But her mom still acts quite strange and Sabrina comes home feeling frustrated about not being able to really talk to her, and confused about which one of them is the parent!

Sabrina feels angry at her mom for not being able to be a mom to her, guilty for feeling angry, and guilty for not seeing her more often. Having a parent who is alive but unable to parent you is probably one of the most painful things that can happen.

Jason's dad was an alcoholic and dropped out of Jason's life when Jason was two years old. Jason didn't even remember his dad, and became very attached to his step-dad. When Jason was twelve years old, his dad stopped drinking, got a good job, remarried, and really put his life back together. He wanted Jason to be a part of his new life, so he asked for joint custody and won. Jason lives with his dad about half the time now, but he doesn't really want to. He says he will never forgive his dad for leaving him, and he really wants to live with his mom and stepdad. Jason is angry at his dad, but feels guilty for being angry because his dad loves him so much and is so good to him. He also is very confused about his love feelings. He likes his dad, but feels more attached to his stepdad. And of course, he's not sure if that is normal.

How to Cope

If you have a parent who is mentally ill or alcoholic, you most likely have many confusing feelings: anger, embarrassment, disappointment, frustration, and guilt. It would probably be a good idea to find someone to talk with honestly about these feelings. Talking would help you to sort the feelings out and to learn that they are normal.

If you were in a position where you were being the parent to your mom or dad, it is important for you to let go of some of that burden. It is *not* your fault that they have a problem and it is not your responsibility to take care of them or to make them okay. In fact, no one can "make them okay." There is help for them in the community, but often the help doesn't work until the sick person is ready to take the initiative in getting it. You have a right to be a kid and an obligation to take care of yourself and to grow and develop into a healthy adult.

If Your Mom or Dad Has Died

Some of you are in a stepfamily because your mom or dad died and your other parent remarried. Having a parent die is a tremendous loss for you, and some kids are as loyal to a dead parent as they are to one that doesn't live with them anymore. That is, they feel like they would be betraying their real mom or dad if they let themselves love a step-mom or stepdad. Sometimes they feel like their lost parent is a traitor for choosing someone else to replace the lost parent. And stepparents sometimes feel like they have to compete with a ghost, or rather an angel, because the dead parent sometimes gets built up to be a perfect, wonderful person, halo and all.

Kids who have lost a parent have said some of the following things about their stepfamilies:

"In some ways, it's a lot easier for us that our dad died. We don't have to hassle with another stepfamily—all the going back and forth, splitting up on holidays, and stuff like that."

"I think it's better because I would hate it if Dad had remarried someone with kids. I know I would feel real jealous of him living with some other kids."

"I think we are more like a regular family than other stepfamilies I know. Our stepdad is our only dad, and we call him 'Dad.' He's all we have, so I think it's easier to get along with him than if I had my real dad, too."

"My stepmom has tried so hard to take the place of our real mom, and sometimes we gave her a real bad time. But I really admire her. She stepped in when she was only twenty-five herself, and gave us all the mothering she could. She is my real mother now, the only mother I will ever really know."

"I used to get real mad at my stepmom and dream that my real mom wouldn't have been so mean. I had her all built up to be a goddess or something. When I got older I started asking my dad what she was really like so that I could get a more realistic picture of her. It turned out that she wasn't perfect. That really helped me accept my step-mom more."

How to Cope

If you still have lots of sad feelings about your parent's death, or if you have a hard time accepting your step-parent, it could be that you need to do some grieving about your loss. Grieving occurs gradually over time and involves other feelings, too, like anger that your parent left you. You can help yourself to deal with these feelings more if you talk with people in your family or another adult about your dead parent and your feelings about him or her dying. Writing about your feelings can also help.

If you have put your dead parent on a pedestal, built up in your mind as being perfect and wonderful, you can get a better perspective by asking questions about that person. You can ask your other parent, your grandparents, or other relatives what your parent was like. You will learn that she or he had faults as well as wonderful qualities, and you may begin to accept the lost parent as a person, not as some sort of god.

If you resent your mom or dad for "replacing" your dead parent by remarrying, you will have to come to accept that your parent has a right to a second chance at marriage and happiness. That doesn't mean that she or he is betraying your dead mom or dad. Most of us need to love and be loved.

If You Don't See Your Sisters, Brothers, or Other Relatives

Some kids are separated from their sisters or brothers, or maybe from a grandparent who was very important to them. This may be because they live far away, or because one of the natural parents has prevented their seeing each other. This can be a very painful situation also, because then you suffer not only the loss of your divorced or dead parent, but also the loss of other significant people in his or her life.

How to Cope

When you are little you don't have any control over this, because the parent with whom you live makes most of your decisions for you. As a teenager, though, you are able to think for yourself, and you have the right to try to reestablish relationships that you have lost.

Talk to your mom or dad and try to explain to them that you want to see or talk to your relative more often. If your parent is willing, offer to earn the money to pay for phone calls and visits yourself.

Find out if people whom you thought had abandoned you really were prevented from seeing you. This often happens with grandparents, aunts, and uncles. If you can't find out from another relative, try to contact the person yourself through a letter or phone call.

If the parent with whom you live is still unwilling to let you see a special grandma or uncle, try to get another adult to help you explain to your mom or dad how important it is for you to see that person. If that doesn't work, you may consider making the contact anyway. It doesn't feel good to do things behind your mom or dad's back, so you might decide to wait until you leave home. If you decide that this is too important to wait for, it is okay to work out a way to do it privately.

Many wonderful relationships have developed after many years of separation, so don't give up hope of seeing a parent or other relative that you have not seen for a long time.

12 * Stepbrothers and Stepsisters

Teenage stepbrothers and stepsisters have mixed feelings about one another. Tom put it this way: "I can't figure my stepsister out. Sometimes when I go there [to her dad's house], Patti's real nice and we have fun together. Other times she's a total bitch. She either complains about everything I do or will hardly talk to me. I don't know what her problem is."

Tom and Patti's love-hate relationship is normal. Teenagers who are brother and sister often have the same mixed feelings about each other and so, of course, stepbrothers and stepsisters will have these mixed feelings, too. And because you are a teenager, you have times when you're moody and depressed and other times when you feel great. So some of Patti's moods have nothing to do with her stepbrother; he just gets the brunt of them because he happens to be around.

It Ain't So Bad

Since there are advantages to having a stepbrother or stepsister, let's talk about that first. It is often easier to talk to a stepsib* about your feelings or problems than a parent because they are near your age and can understand. When you visit your absent parent and there are teenagers there, it makes the visit easier because you can hang out with your stepsibs instead of spending the whole time with your parents.

If you live with your stepbrother or stepsister, then you probably help each other out now and then: loan money, give a ride, trade chores, etc. If you have been an only child, it may be a little less lonely having a stepbrother or stepsister to talk with and fight with! If your stepsib is younger, he or she probably thinks you're the greatest because you're older, and that's good for your ego.

If your stepsib is a different sex than you, he or she can help you learn and understand more about how guys or girls think or feel. A stepsib can also be a good source of advice.

Sharing Your Parent

"My dad has four stepdaughters. One of them is near my age, and I feel like my dad has replaced me with Stacy. So when I go there I feel really jealous of her and get so mad at her I could strangle her. She's really sweet, but that doesn't have anything to do with it." Wendy talked about her feelings with a mixture of embarrassment and anger. These are really very normal feelings. It's hard to see your absent parent living with someone who is not your mom or dad, and with a bunch of kids who are not your sisters or brothers. And it's upsetting to realize that those kids get to see your dad or mom every day and you don't. No wonder you feel jealous and sometimes hateful toward your stepbrothers and sisters. As normal as these feelings

* Stepsibs: short for stepsiblings, meaning stepbrothers or stepsisters.

(104)

are, they are negative and unpleasant for you to feel, so let's look at some things you can do to feel better.

How to Cope

Remind yourself over and over that your absent parent is in a situation that is probably his or her second choice. Your parent's first choice would be to live with you. Because of the divorce, that is absolutely not possible. So you have to live apart, and they hate it as much as you do. We've talked to a lot of remarried people and never met any who were glad to be away from their kids. They were glad to have their unhappy marriages over, but they felt sick about being separated from their kids. Remember, also, that your parent did not choose those kids! He or she chose the new spouse, and the kids were part of the package. Your stepsisters and brothers didn't choose your mom or dad as a parent, either. They had no say in the matter, and may feel as helpless as you do. In fact, they would probably much rather be living with both their natural parents and give you your natural parent back!

Talking about your feelings can sometimes make them less troublesome. If, for instance, you feel real jealous of your stepsister, you might consider telling her how you feel. This would probably accomplish several things:

1. You will feel better because you've said out loud what's bothering you.

2. Your stepbrother might be able to understand you better if you tell him what's going on with you. The chances are pretty good that if you're jealous of your stepbrother you are kind of mean to him sometimes and he probably doesn't understand why.

3. Your stepsister may share some of her feelings with you that will help you to feel better. She may be having a hard time accepting your dad, and feel very uncomfortable with the situation herself. You can probably say

things to her that would help her understand your dad better.

4. One of the magic things about sharing your feelings honestly with someone else is that you end up feeling closer to the person you share your feelings with, and less resentful toward them.

5. It would be a good idea to tell your absent parent how you feel, too.

How Not to Say It

"It must be nice to get everything you want. My dad never buys me three shirts at once."

To Dad: "Geez, you really spoil Tim and Andy, don't you? They get to do everything with you."

How to Say It

"Stacy, it's hard to tell you this, but sometimes I feel real jealous of you because my dad buys you nice clothes."

"Dad, sometimes I feel real real jealous of Tim and Andy because they get to see you every day and do things with you and I don't."

Shifting Roles

Another difficult thing about living with or visiting with stepsibs is that your role in the family changes. One of your most secure roles comes from your birth order—where you were born in relation to your brothers and sisters. For example, if you were the oldest child in your first family, your role was probably "the responsible oldest one." There is status and security knowing just how you fit in. When you visit your stepsibs, you may suddenly be displaced by an older stepsib. You may feel that you don't know how to act, or even who you are!

[106]

Jenny, twelve, was the "baby" of her family. She had two older brothers who did most of the work around the house, and Jenny usually got off the hook. Everyone took care of her, and she felt secure and special. When Jenny went to her dad's for the summer, she was suddenly the oldest child! Her dad and stepmother expected her to help with her six-year-old stepbrother and her new baby half-sister. They were on her case a lot for not finishing a job, picking up her things, or for not being as responsible as they thought she should be! Jenny spent the first week of her visit in tears, until she got used to NOT being the baby. Needless to say, she grew up a lot that first summer.

Feeling Like an Outsider and Feeling Like You've Been Invaded

Whenever you have stepsibs that you visit or live with, you may feel one of two ways. If your stepsibs visit you or move in with you, you will feel as though they are invading your territory. You probably often think it would be just great if they would go away. If you visit your stepsibs at their house, or move into their house, *you* will probably feel like an outsider. Neither role is much fun.

Joe, thirteen, tells what it's like to feel invaded. "When my mom married Dan, and he moved in with us, it wasn't too bad. He was pretty nice to us and fit in with our family okay. But last year Dan's son, Eric, came to live with us and he still doesn't really fit in. He feels like company that doesn't know when to go home. We had to totally rearrange our house to make room for him. I had to give up my room and move in with my brother, Jack [Jack is 16]. It's more crowded when we go someplace in the car. My mom and Dan both got stricter about what time we go to bed, when we come home, when we do our jobs, everything. You see, Eric is sort of wild, so my parents made all these rules to help shape him up, but it's not fair to Jack

and me. Eric isn't used to doing any chores, so we all suffer because he usually does a lousy job. I feel sorry for
Eric because he has problems and his mom kicked him
out, but he ruined everything and I hate him being here."

Kathy, who is fourteen, is the outsider in her family.
She and her mom moved into her stepdad's house, where
he had been living with his three teenage children. Kathy
says, "I don't feel like I'll ever belong here. It's their house
and they make sure I know it every chance they get. I'm
afraid to even make a snack for myself without feeling like
I'm stealing their food. If I take a towel it's the wrong one.
Sometimes, I'll start to get close to one of my stepsisters,
usually Angie. [Angie is fourteen also.] I think Angie and I
could be friends. We really have fun together, but as soon
as we get together, one of the other kids horns in and sort
of gets Angie to go back on their side. I think Angie has to
take sides with her own sister and brother because they
are more important to her than I am."

A lot of the problems that Joe and Kathy describe
could be avoided if new families could start out in a new
home. Then everyone would start out on equal footing
rather than with one feeling invaded and one feeling like
an outsider. Unfortunately, most of us can't afford to go
out and buy a new house when we remarry, so usually one
family moves in with the other family, and it takes a lot of
work and open talking about feelings to resolve the out-
sider/invader problem.

Kathy's problem about getting close to her stepsister
Angie is a common problem also. Your real brothers and
sisters are always going to be a little jealous if you be-
friend the outsider, and they may do things to get you back
on their side. Try not to give in to their pressure. Your new
stepbrother or stepsister really needs a friend, and you
are helping your whole family out when you're nice to a
stepsib.

How to Cope

Try to promote a family meeting so that all the kids get a chance to sit down and talk about their own "personal rules," like whether they want others to knock before coming in their room, or whether they are willing to share their records or tapes. We are not very good mind-readers about other people's rules, and violations of these rules are what cause most of the problems between stepsiblings.

If you are an outsider, try to understand that your stepsibs are going to feel very touchy about their personal belongings and rules. Ask direct questions like, "Is this shampoo yours or is it for everyone to use?" or "Do you want me to ask before I play your guitar?" or "When do you usually take your shower?"

If you are the insider, try to respect the fact that the outsider does not know all the millions of little family rules that you take for granted. Don't be afraid to tell your stepbrother or stepsister all the things about how the house is run. Be sure to ask about what they like in the way of privacy, too, or what personal belongings they don't want you to use.

A cardinal rule for outsiders and insiders is this: *never* borrow or use anything belonging to your stepsib without asking, whether it's clothing, musical instruments, stereos, radios, bicycles, or cars. If you are not sure whether or not something is privately owned or shared by the whole family, *ask!*

The Insider Can Feel Like an Outsider, Too

We've noticed that sooner or later everyone in a stepfamily has times when they feel like they don't belong, that they are an outsider. The McNeil teenagers explain what it's like in their family. Melanie lives with her mother in another part of the state, while her brother, Bill, lives with their father, his second wife, and her daughter, Audrey. When Melanie visits two or three times a year she feels like a guest rather than a member of the family because, she says, "The family doesn't behave in the same way when I'm there." It turns out that Melanie isn't the only one who feels out of it when she comes to visit. Audrey feels like an outsider because her stepbrother, Bill, and stepsister, Melanie, spend a lot of time together and are very close. Bill has his own problems, because he doesn't want to hurt his stepsister's feelings but he does want to spend a lot of special time with his own sister.

Each of the McNeil kids copes with his or her feelings in a different way. Because Melanie wants to be a part of the family and to be accepted, she is a "good girl"—very helpful, very nice to every one, and she never makes waves. Audrey deals with feeling left out by getting very quiet and spending a lot of time with her own friends. Bill copes with his pressures by getting crabby.

If you feel left out when you're around your stepbrothers and stepsisters, you may feel powerless to change the situation, and in a way you are right. Biological brothers and sisters usually feel closer to each other than to a stepsib. But there are some things you can do so you won't feel so lonely and left out.

How to Cope

This will sound risky to you, but we think it will help if you tell your stepbrother or stepsister that you feel left out. They probably don't have any idea you feel that way and would want to know. They can't make an effort to include you more unless they know you feel excluded.

If you've tried that and nothing changes, then remind yourself that there's nothing wrong with you. You're not a creep just because they are closer to one another than they are to you. Try to accept the situation without feeling real bitter, and focus your efforts on other relationships. Spend more time with friends, parents, and other people. If you are happy with other relationships, you won't feel so left out and hurt.

Whose Friends Are Whose?

When Rick's stepbrother was visiting, his mom overheard him making up an excuse to a friend on the phone. She asked him about it, and he told her the guys were going to have a football game down at the park and had asked him to come along. She asked him why he didn't go and take his stepbrother with him (both boys were fifteen), and Rick said he didn't feel like it. Now, Rick's mom knew he never passes up a football game with his friends, so she asked him more about it later. Rick had to think for a while, and then he said, "Mom, I don't want my friends to meet Dean. He's bigger than I am and probably better at football than I am, and what if my friends like him better than they do me?"

Part of being the one "invaded" means that you may have to share your friends with your stepsib. That's real hard for most kids to do, because they're afraid that they'll lose their friends to the "invader." The outsider, on the other hand, doesn't quite know if it's okay to try to get into the same group of friends his or her stepsib has, or to stay away from that group, and try to make totally new friends. Either way is hard, and there can be lots of jealous feelings between stepsibs about their friends.

How to Cope

If you are able to share your friends with your stepsib in the beginning, there is a pretty good chance that, after awhile, they will wind up having completely different friends than you have. Most stepsibs that we know are not really interested in the same friends because they are so different from one another. So meeting your friends is just a way of starting, and through your friends, they will probably meet other kids.

Whether you are the one being invaded or the outsider, it will help if the two of you can talk about this ahead of time and express your concerns and try to make a plan.

If you are the one being invaded, you can help your stepsib to make different friends than yours by introducing him or her to people who have the same interests, or by telling him about the different clubs and activities at your school.

Try to refrain from "putting down" each other's friends. That often occurs out of jealousy and is not good for either one of you.

Sexual Attraction

A common problem for teenage stepbrothers and stepsisters is sexual attraction. Lisa, fifteen, has two stepbrothers, one her own age and one two years older. They don't live in the same house with her, but since both her stepbrothers are "foxes," she gets attracted to one or the other now and then. Lisa's parents realize her attraction is perfectly normal, because she and her stepbrothers are not related. So they have never made a big deal out of it.

Things get a little stickier if you are attracted to a stepbrother or stepsister you live with. Again, this is absolutely normal, and you are not a "sicky" if you feel this way. The question is what to do about your feelings. We go into this problem in depth in the next chapter, so be sure to read it. What most kids do about their feelings of attraction is to try to deny them to themselves, feel guilty, and then find a way to get more distance between themselves and the person they're turned on to. The way a lot of kids make distance is to begin picking fights with their stepsibs or by putting them down all the time.

How to Cope

If you are giving your stepsister or stepbrother a bad time, check out with yourself whether or not you're attracted to him or her. If you think you might be, don't panic. These are perfectly normal feelings. You might think about handling them in a way that's not so unpleasant for both of you. It takes two to fight and you may able to reduce the amount of fighting by pulling out more often.

Developing a good, talking friendship is a good way to deal with that attraction. Often it goes away as you get to know the other person better.

Try spending more time with people outside the family—either by getting more involved with your friends or school activities, or by pursuing friends of the opposite sex.

Avoid being alone in the house with your stepsib. Invite a friend over more often. And try to cut out any sexy or provocative behavior on your part.

If your feelings just won't go away then discuss it with your mom or dad. They may be able to arrange your family situation so you and your stepsib are not thrown together so much.

Read the chapter on sex for more about this problem.

Arguing

When people live together they fight. Some fight a little, others fight a lot, but everyone fights. In first families the kids start fighting as soon as they are both old enough to want the same toy, and the fighting continues till they are adults. At the same time, though, a bond of love and affection is developing between the kids so their relationship is balanced between caring and fighting. When you move in with a stepbrother or stepsister, you don't have this bond of affection and history. In fact, you may hardly know one another. All of a sudden you have a new sister or brother, and it's a shock! Because you have different values and different ways of doing things, you're going to disagree and argue.

How to Cope

"Differences are okay." If you're fighting with your stepbrother or stepsister, try to remember that differences aren't necessarily good or bad, and that one way of doing something isn't better than the other. You just approach things differently. In the McNeil family, Bill loves acid rock and Rosie likes jazz. Their different tastes in music aren't a problem until one or the other turns up the stereo so loud that the other is forced to listen to the "gruesome" music. Then all hell breaks loose.

Try making a deal, or looking for a solution to the problem that is okay with both sides. Bill and Rosie worked out their stereo problem by agreeing not to turn it up above a certain number when the other was home. When the other's not home, each listens to it as loud as they wish.

If you share a bathroom with your stepsib and you both want to use it at the same time every day, see if you can work out a deal where one gets it first one day and the other gets it first the next day. Agree to stay in the bathroom for only half an hour and agree not to bang on the door while the other's in there.

One way to decrease your fights with your stepbrother or stepsister is to decide whether or not something your stepsib is doing affects your life or whether it's really not your business. For instance, your stepsister bor-

[114]

rows your clothes and doesn't return them; this clearly affects you. On the other hand, let's say your stepbrother pigs out before dinner and then picks at his dinner. His behavior is kind of irritating, but it really doesn't affect you directly and is therefore none of your business. A guideline would be that if it affects you, you have the right to comment on it; if it doesn't, mind your own business and let it go.

When You Don't Like Your Stepbrother or Stepsister

Sometimes stepbrothers and stepsisters just plain don't like each other. If you happen to be not very fond of your stepsister or stepbrother, that's not particularly surprising. After all, you didn't choose this person to be a relative; they just came along with your stepparent. You probably couldn't live with some of your friends and still like them very well either. Your stepbrother or stepsister may have very different values than you, or may behave in an obnoxious way when you're together and so it's just not possible for you to like him or her. That's okay.

Todd, eighteen, just hated it when his fourteen-year-old stepsister, Tracy, came for her annual summer visit. Todd's mother and stepfather would turn themselves inside out trying to make everything just perfect for Tracy the whole time she was there. Todd felt like a second-class citizen, detested Tracy, and referred to her sarcastically as "the little princess." In this case, Todd's loathing of his stepsister was not so much because she was awful but because his parents played favorites when she was around.

In a counseling session, Todd finally told his parents how he felt. At first they felt defensive and thought Todd was being a baby, but they finally came to understand his feelings and felt very bad about what they had been doing. Todd's mom also realized how hard she had been trying to make Tracy like her, mostly to win her husband's approval. She understood how much tension this created for everyone and how unfair it had been to Todd. The following summer when Tracy came, everyone was a bit more relaxed and Tracy was treated more like one of the family rather than a visiting princess. Todd found it much easier to tolerate her and was more comfortable with the situation.

How to Cope

See if you can figure out how why you don't like your stepsib. If it's just a personality clash or if your stepsib acts like a complete idiot when you're together, there's not a lot you can do to change your feelings. You will feel better about yourself, though, if you can manage at least to be civil and polite.

Occasionally, like Todd, intense dislike can come from feeling jealous of your stepbrother or stepsister or feeling like you have to compete for your natural parent. Talking to your mom or dad about this and getting some reassurance or more fair treatment can help you to feel less jealous and to feel better about your stepsib.

Try to keep the lines of communication open between you and your stepsib so that you can talk about the things they do that really bug you and solve some of the problems. That will help to keep the tension down. Family meetings are a good place to talk to a stepsister or stepbrother that you don't like very much. (See Appendix I, "How to Hold a Family Council.")

If you are the one that's not liked, try not to take it personally. Your stepsib may have liked you under different circumstances, but when you are in the same stepfamily, it becomes very complicated. He or she may never be able to accept you, for some of the reasons we have discussed in this chapter.

13 * Sex in Your Stepfamily

We think it is important to discuss the sexual feelings in stepfamilies very openly. Sex is difficult for many people to talk about, and in families, especially, sexual feelings or problems are frequently swept under the rug. That may be okay in regular families, but in stepfamilies where there are teenagers, sexual feelings are strong, and sometimes can lead to some very serious problems.

It is hard for adults to accept that teenagers are very sexual people, that they spend much more time thinking about sex and experiencing sexual feelings than do adults. Since all of us adults were teenagers once, it's hard to understand why we don't recognize how sexual you are!

Our purpose is not to provide you with your sex education, but we think it would be helpful to review some basic facts about your adolescent development.

When boys and girls mature physically, they develop a strong interest in the opposite sex. New sexual thoughts and activities are perfectly normal. A girl usually matures around twelve or thirteen, and although she develops an interest in the opposite sex then, she usually does not have a need to get together sexually with boys until later.

Boys mature a year or two later than girls, at about fourteen or fifteen. Usually, within a year after his body starts to change, a boy will have his first ejaculation. Although ejaculation is a normal sign of puberty for boys, the sex education you get at school does not often include this fact. So when boys start ejaculating (usually through masturbation or wet dreams at first), they often have a lot of guilt. For a boy, the teenage years are the most sexual time of his life. The average high school boy has more orgasms than his teachers or parents! Girls are very sexual as teenagers also, but they usually don't become sexually active until a little later.

Parents sometimes don't want to accept you as being sexually mature, and they are more concerned with the "don'ts" than with helping you understand your drives. In stepfamilies with teenagers, problems that have to do with sex are much more obvious and harder to ignore, but there is not much help with these problems since they are so hard to talk about. We will discuss some of the problems we have seen in the stepfamilies we have talked with.

Living With a Single Parent Forces You to Recognize Your Parent's Sexuality

In your original family, you probably could ignore the fact that your parents were sexual people. Most kids just don't like to think about their parents having sex. Some kids are sure that the only time their parents had sex was when each child was conceived. Parents in this culture don't act sexy around their kids and usually keep their sexual activities quite secret, so it is no wonder that kids have a hard time imagining their mom and dad having sex.

Then, when your parents were divorced, each of them most likely started dating. You may remember the way you felt when a strange man came to your house to pick up your mom for a date, or when your dad brought his girlfriend along when he took you somewhere. Besides all the jealous feelings, and the feelings of loyalty about the parent that was being replaced, you also may have found yourself wondering what they did when they were alone! Maybe you saw Mom or Dad acting really lovey with a date. Perhaps they touched each other a lot or always sat real close or hugged and kissed in front of you or acted really silly. This behavior may have made you feel angry or disgusted with them. There was probably a time when you suspected that they were sleeping together. Maybe you heard your mother's boyfriend leave early in the morning, or maybe your mom or dad didn't come home until 2:00 or 3:00 a.m.

A lot of the painful feelings you had during those times had to do with your coping with the fact that your mom or dad may have been having sex, and probably enjoying it! A fifteen-year-old told us once, "They're so old! Why would they want to have sex with each other?"

If you are a girl, you may have had an especially difficult time accepting that your mother is interested in sex! You are in the middle of your own search for identity, trying to figure out who you are and whether you are comfortable with your own sexual feelings and behavior, and your mother, your main role model, sensible and nonsexual, starts acting in very weird ways. There are lots of mixed messages that you have gotten about being sexual. TV, magazines, books, and the movies are full of sexy girls, but the message from your parents, school, and community says that you are supposed to be "good," "wholesome," and in general nonsexual. This is a very confusing time for you, and watching Mom act like a teenager may be very upsetting to you.

If you are a boy, your reactions are probably somewhat different. You may feel very protective about your mother, and certainly just as upset when you see her going out. You may feel furious at her boyfriend, and at her if you see her acting in suggestive ways. Your feelings may be more those of jealousy or protectiveness toward her. Usually young adolescent boys have some sexual feelings toward their own mothers, but because of the "sex taboo" you may not even notice those feelings or admit them to

(119)

yourself. So when your mom starts dating other men, you may feel quite angry.

Both boys and girls have similar feelings about their dads, but the feelings are usually not quite as strong. There is more permission in our society for men to be sexual, and they generally talk, think, and act in slightly more "promiscuous" ways, like enjoying "girlie" magazines like *Playboy* or *Penthouse*. Girls will still be jealous of their dad's girlfriend, and boys may be angry at their dad for being obviously sexual.

Remarriage

When your mom or dad remarries, the situation may be very uncomfortable for you. Your parent and stepparent may be more openly affectionate with each other and, worse yet, may go in their room and close the door more often. They may also go away for the weekend more frequently. There is no way for you to ignore that these people have sex together! Maybe quite frequently! You may feel uncomfortable with their intimacy, jealous of their relationship, or confused by feelings of loyalty for your other parent.

How to Cope

Recognize that jealous, protective feelings toward your mom or dad are perfectly normal.

Try to accept that you will never have your mom or your dad all to yourself. They are adults and they will always have important adult relationships. They know that you will be gone in a few years and that they will need a good life without you.

Spend more time with your own friends and people your own age. It is easy to get too involved with what is going on at home during this time.

If your feelings are so painful that you can't study or that you withdraw from your friends, find an adult to talk to about your feelings. If you don't know one that you trust that much, ask your parents to find a counselor for you.

Teenagers Are Often Sexually Attracted to Their Stepmom or Stepdad

Since teenagers are so sexual, they are capable of appreciating any attractive person of the opposite sex. At one time or another, you may have been attracted to a teacher or other adult that you like. We accept those "crushes" as being a normal teenage experience. Stepparents are no exception. And it's easier to feel sexy about a stepparent than, say, a natural parent, because the rules about sexuality between people who are not related are looser than for those who are.

You learned at a very young age that it was not okay to have any sexual feelings about your natural parent. That is what the "incest taboo" is, an unspoken rule that there is to be no sexual activity within a family, except between the husband and wife. The only way that families can stay together and raise healthy and productive children is if it is very clear that there is to be no sex between parents and children or between brothers and sisters. This unspoken rule is so strong that you probably never even were aware of any sexual attraction to your mom, dad, or brothers and sisters. If you did have those feelings, you probably felt very guilty about them or hid them even from yourself.

There is no incest taboo about stepparents, though, because you are not biologically related. You may find yourself as attracted to a stepparent as you are to a favorite teacher. These feelings may cause problems in a stepfamily. You may feel very ashamed for having these feelings and may act in some strange ways. You may find that

[121]

you withdraw from your family, spend more time with friends, and in general try to stay away from the person who provokes thoses feelings in you. You may find yourself being very hostile and angry toward your stepparent, without even realizing what you are doing. You may argue a lot or, in general, be really difficult to be around. What you are trying to do, although you may not even be aware of it, is to stay away from that person and fool yourself and everyone else about your feelings. But sexual thoughts and fantasies are natural and are *not* the same as actions.

Stepparents are human too, and being human, they are also sexual. Sometimes they are attracted to a stepchild, as well. Joy went to live with her mother and her stepfather when she was only ten years old. She and her stepfather fought about almost everything as Joy grew up. If Joy wasn't mad at Bert, Bert was mad at Joy. Their relationship was very loud. Finally, when Joy was about seventeen, her stepfather and she had some major differences of opinion. Bert felt that it was time for Joy to move out. They were in some family therapy at the time, and one day Bert and Joy were having a session alone with the therapist to try and figure out what to do. Bert confessed during that session that he had been attracted to Joy ever since she began to mature sexually and that he found those feelings irritating. He had known for many years that his anger at Joy was partly to keep her distant from him, and now, he confessed, it would be much easier on him if she left home. When Joy heard this, she confessed also that she had been attracted to Bert from the time she started maturing and having sexual feelings. She thought he was very foxy and sexy and was jealous of her mother's relationship with him. It was hard for Joy to admit those feelings even to herself. She realized that she was hateful to Bert for the same reason that he was always angry with her. They were both trying to keep their distance from her. They were both trying to keep their distance from each other and deal with some very difficult feelings. They agreed that it would be better if Joy moved out of the house, and they agreed that it would be very hurtful and unnecessary to tell Joy's mother what they had discovered. They both had had so many guilty feelings over the years that it helped them each in their own lives to get that stuff out in the open.

The situation that Bert and Joy were in is a fairly common one. Usually, each person is totally unaware that the other is sexually attracted. Not too long ago, a young stepmother named Lois came to talk with us. She was troubled because her nineteen-year-old stepson was withdrawing and acting distant and hostile. She said he had been acting noticeably different for about six months. We asked if Jeff, her stepson, had a girlfriend. She said he had broken up with his last girlfriend about six months ago and had not really dated anyone since. We asked Lois if she had ever considered that Jeff might be having sexual feelings about her. Lois was an extremely attractive young woman. She said that was a ridiculous idea, that she had been Jeff's stepmother for about eight years, had been close to him and loved him like a son. When we asked about their living situation, it turned out that they lived in a small house with only one bathroom, and that she and her husband were very casual about running around in towels or underwear, and that everyone in the house was very comfortable with that. Because of her own motherly feelings toward Jeff, it was very hard for Lois to imagine that she was probably driving Jeff wild with her semi-nudity. A few weeks later, she told us that she and her husband had discussed what we had suggested and that her husband admitted he had been feeling Jeff's discomfort with Lois's casual bathroom manner, but was afraid to say anything to her about it. They also noticed that when Jeff had a girlfriend, he was able to treat Lois in a nicer way than when he didn't have a girlfriend. They wondered if when Jeff had a girlfriend he had an outlet for his sexual feelings and could feel safer with Lois than when he had no other object for his sexual feelings. We suspect they were right on with their observation. The point of this story is that adults usually underestimate the sexuality in young people and, without meaning to, act in inappropriate ways.

Sexual incidents take place more frequently between stepdaughter and stepfather than between stepson and stepmother. When a teenage girl is presented with a new stepfather, she may not know exactly how to behave with him. She may behave in a flirty or provocative way, just because she is in the process of trying to figure out how to relate to people of the opposite sex in a way that will make her attractive to them. That same behavior may have been real safe when she tried it out on her real father, because he loves her in a special way. Her real father may respond to her with affection or think she's real cute, but usually will ignore any slightly sexual behavior. A stepfather, on the other hand, has no history of parent-child stuff with this girl/woman, and may get turned on, or may not understand that his job is to help her define the relationship in an appropriate way.

How to Cope

If your problem is that you feel sexually attracted to your stepparent or you fantasize about him or her, recognize that these are normal feelings and not dangerous in themselves.

Recognize and accept that you will never be able to act on these feelings. You may find someone just like your stepparent, but you cannot ever have him or her. Your stepparent belongs to your mother or father and their relationship is what will make or break your stepfamily. If your feelings are very strong, like Joy's, and you are old enough to move out of your home, do so. Both you and your family will be more comfortable.

Sexual Assault

Most stepdads do great in their new role. But don't forget that they grew up to appreciate feminine beauty in all its forms. Some men fail to handle their feelings in a healthy way, and the incidence of stepfathers sexually assaulting teenage daughters, and even younger girls, is appallingly high. Sometimes the girl has provoked the assault by parading around half dressed or acting in other sexy ways around her stepfather, and other times she has done absolutely nothing. There is never a good enough excuse for an adult male to sexually approach a teenage female, no matter how sexy she behaves. Stepfathers who participate sexually with their stepdaughters are always maladjusted, immature, or desperately in need of professional help. It is inappropriate behavior and ultimately destructive to your emotional and sexual development and to your family.

When Julie was about twelve, her stepdad, Paul, started to hug her a lot and kiss her on the lips. Julie felt uncomfortable about it, but wasn't sure if there was anything wrong with what he was doing. They had had a close, affectionate relationship for about five years. Paul had always come in her room at night, and kissed her on the forehead, but now he began to fondle her breasts or her buttocks. Julie would pretend she was asleep. Gradually Paul started lying down beside her, rubbing up against her and touching her more and more. Julie could not pretend she was asleep any longer; she pulled away and said "no" or "please stop." Paul started talking to Julie in a loving way and telling her it was okay, that he loved her and would never hurt her, and that he wanted her to learn about sex from someone who loved her. This went on until Julie was sixteen. Often she would go into the bathroom and throw up after her dad left her room. She told her mom once that her stepdad came into her room and her mom said she

(125)

must have been dreaming. Julie was afraid to tell anyone else. She did care about Paul and didn't want to get him in trouble, and she knew her mother could not support herself and Julie financially without his help.

Finally, one day, Julie shared her secret with her girlfriend, Dee. Dee got very upset and convinced Julie to confide in Dee's mom. Dee's mom wanted to call a child abuse agency, but Julie was afraid. Together, they called one of the local hotlines and, without using any names, talked to a counselor there. He suggested that Dee's mother help Julie talk to her mom about it. He offered to talk to Julie's mom also, if they wanted to call back. With this support, Julie was able to convince her mom about what was going on.

Julie took some clothes and went to stay at Dee's house, and her mom confronted Paul when he came home from work. At first he denied it, but finally he broke down and cried and admitted what he was doing. Julie's mom called the child abuse unit and she and Paul both went in to talk to a counselor. After expressing her rage and her guilt, Julie's mom agreed to go with Paul to marriage counseling and try to figure out why this had happened to their family. Paul was also required to go to group therapy with other men who were sexually assaulting someone. Julie lived with Dee and her family for about nine months. She went to family counseling with her mom and stepdad for several months before she moved back home.

How to Cope

If there is anything that your stepfather does that seems too sexy or makes you feel uncomfortable, tell him to stop. You have the right to protect yourself. You do not always have to do what adults say if you know it is wrong. Sometimes just speaking up or threatening to tell someone stops what's going on. You may want to get a lock for your bedroom door.

Make sure that you are acting in appropriate ways around your stepfather. Even though you may not think so, you may look like you are asking for his sexual attention.

If you are being assaulted or have been assaulted, be sure to tell your mom or another adult. Don't let it go on. Your family needs help and they will get it only if your mom or other adult contacts the proper authorities. It's very hard to "turn in" your own stepdad, but these days he will not be thrown in jail, he will have to go to counseling and get help and either you or he will live away from home for a while.

Remind yourself that your stepdad's behavior is *not* your fault and you do not have to feel guilty about what happens to him. It is important that you take care of yourself, and allowing an adult to sexually abuse you is not taking care of yourself.

Read Chapter 9 about "Mr. Hotpants."

Do Stepmothers Assault Their Stepsons?

Some stepmothers do behave in a seductive way with their stepsons. This behavior can include parading around half-dressed in front of him, touching and carressing him a lot, or simply moving her body in a sexy way when talking with him. This behavior can be very difficult emotionally for a teenage boy, because he may become infatuated with his stepmom and not spend time with girls his own age, or he may have secret wishes about getting his father out of the way and feel guilty about that.

Occasionally we have heard of a stepmother actually seducing her stepson or directly letting him know that she's open to his advances. This situation is loaded with mixed feelings of guilt and confusion for stepmother and stepson, and can threaten the survival of the family.

Stepmothers and teenagers who are involved in this kind of a relationship emotionally or physically need help in sorting out their feelings and clarifying what is appropriate for them.

How to Cope

If your stepmother appears to be coming on to you, try to find a private time to tell her how uncomfortable her behavior is making you feel. It's OK to get angry in order to get yourself to tell her this.

It is not in your best interest to respond to your stepmother's advances no matter how neat you think she is! Try to ignore her or try to spend more time with your friends. Having a physical relationship with your stepmother will cause you nothing but grief, and may delay your own social development.

If you become hopelessly confused about your feelings or if you are having a sexual relationship with your stepmother get some help for yourself immediately! See a counselor at school or ask your dad if you can see a therapist.

Feelings between Teenage Stepbrothers and Stepsisters Can also Be Troublesome

When attractive teenage boys and girls begin to live together, share a bathroom, and see each other every day, it is unlikely that their relationship is going to be completely brotherly or sisterly. One or the other of them is most likely going to feel attracted to or get a "crush" on the other. These feelings usually pass as you get to know one another better and see each other's faults.

Toni and her mom moved in with Bob and his kids

when Toni was thirteen and in the eighth grade. Bob's son, Roger, was sixteen and really thought Toni was great. He loved having this cute, sexy girl living in his own house. He would help her with her homework, and take her with him when he ran an errand. Toni was naturally very flattered by all this attention and really looked up to Roger. She always would sit close to Roger in the car or when they were watching TV. She began ignoring her own brother, Joe, and spent whatever time she could with Roger. This complicated matters further, because Joe felt completely left out and hurt that his sister liked her new brother more, and he resented Roger for taking over his role as an older brother.

The parents thought it was great that Toni and Roger hit it off so well, and they were so preoccupied with their own new marriage that it never occurred to them that anything was going on between Toni and Roger. One day, though, Toni's mom walked into the TV room unexpectedly and found Toni and Roger snuggled up in the bean bag chair together. Toni's mom was pretty upset, mostly at herself for not being aware of what was going on. She suddenly realized that Roger and Toni had often arranged to stay home alone together. She did speak to Toni, however, and told Toni that it was not okay to have Roger for a boyfriend, and that she was concerned that Toni didn't really know what she was getting into. Toni admitted to her mom that she was getting a little scared about the way that Roger wanted to touch her and kiss her. Toni listened to her mom, and began to pull away from Roger. (Her mom helped her figure out things to say.) Before too long Roger started going with a girl from school and started paying less attention to Toni. Roger and Toni lived together for about three more years, and still are good friends, so in this family, those feelings worked themselves out.

Sometimes it's not quite that easy, however, and then all the people involved do have to sit down and figure out what to do. Occasionally other living arrangements have to be made because most parents will not allow children living under their roof to be in a boyfriend-girlfriend relationship with each other. It is too complicated for everyone involved and can be very destructive to your family as a unit.

Sometimes teenagers are sexually attracted to each other, but those feelings are not really conscious, and the teenagers fool themselves by fighting a lot or acting really mean to each other. When you act opposite to the way you really feel, we call that "defensive" behavior. We all do defensive things when we don't want to face our own feelings. In this case, it would be really scary to admit to yourself that you have sexual feelings about a stepbrother or stepsister, so you may act a little bit like the third grader who hits a girl because he likes her.

How to Cope

Recognize that sexual feelings toward a stepbrother or stepsister are perfectly normal feelings, but it is out of the question to act out any of those feelings while one or both of you is living in your family home. Other brothers and sisters would get jealous and protective and everyone would be fighting all the time. And what happens when you want to break up?

If the feelings of infatuation don't pass as you get to know each other better, talk to your parents or another adult about this problem.

If you get scared about your stepsister or stepbrother coming on to you and you don't know how to handle it, be sure to talk to your mom or dad. Your parents will want to help protect you from any sexual advances that you are not mature enough yet to deal with.

If the problem gets too big to handle, you may want to suggest that one of you live with the other parent or with another relative.

If you and your stepsister or stepbrother truly decide

that you love each other and want to be together, tell yourself that that can always happen after you both leave the family home. What you do then is basically your own business.

14 * Parents in a Homosexual Relationship

No one knows for sure how many kids have parents who have switched from being straight, or heterosexual, to gay. Since about 10 percent of all the human population is homosexual, a guess is that between 1 and 2 percent make this switch in adulthood. If you have a parent who has made this change, you are having very special stepparent problems that we will talk about in this chapter.

Why a Parent "Changes" From Straight to Gay

When a teenager learns that his or her parent has gone from being a "normal," straight person to a homosexual, it can be one of the most upsetting things in the world. Most kids ask, "Why did you do this to me?"

A switch in sexual preference is fairly complicated. In almost all cases these people were born with their sexual preference already decided for them: they were born gay. Their liking for the same sex was not something they chose or had any control over; it just existed as part of them since birth, like the color of their eyes or whether they grew to be short or tall.

As they were growing up, they got a million messages from our culture that it was wrong, evil, dirty, sinful and bad to have sexual feelings for the same sex. Because it was "wrong" to feel sexual attraction for the same sex, they decided to ignore as much as possible any homosexual feelings. That took a lot of strength and determination, because it meant denying a very strong urge almost every day. It's like trying to pretend you're not hungry when you're starved.

Over the years such people almost talked themselves out of the fact of being gay and worked at developing sexual feelings for the opposite sex. For a long time that was successful; they were turned on by people of the opposite sex, dated, eventually married, and had kids. For a long while they felt safe, having fooled themselves and the rest of the world into believing they were heterosexual. But over time their natural and inborn attraction for the same sex began surfacing again and they became pretty uncomfortable. They faced the awful decision of whether to keep pretending everything was okay when it wasn't, or of choosing to live their life honestly and in a way that is normal and right for them as homosexuals.

Becoming aware that you are homosexual can be a terrible crisis, often the worst time in your life, because of the decisions necessary. Some people handle this well and are in fact relieved to admit to themselves and others that they are gay, but many others get scared and depressed.

Some parents resolve their problem by staying in their marriages and having homosexual affairs on the side. These people and others who have not acknowledged their homosexuality publicly are called "closet gays." If your parent is in an openly gay relationship, she or he has "come out of the closet" and announced to the world the change in sexual partners and life-style. This was a scary transition for your parent and very upsetting for you. Most gay people feel good about being gay once they have acknowledged it and accepted it. Their primary problem remains other people's inability to accept their homosexuality.

Feeling Angry at Your Parent and His or Her Lover

When your parent admitted to being gay (or when you discovered it), you probably experienced many emotions: shock, disbelief, betrayal, hurt, sadness, depression, embarrassment, anger. These are all normal feelings, and you should not feel guilty that you feel these and many other emotions from time to time. After all, you probably feel your parent pulled a very dirty trick on you, and you will react with strong emotions. Some kids are not all that upset by their parents being gay and adjust rather easily. Other kids think they are not upset, but begin to fail in school, get in trouble with drugs, or begin having other problems.

Jane came into counseling because she was very concerned about the way her three teenagers were reacting to the fact that she had become a lesbian. Jane is an outgoing, warm, and funny woman who was married for twelve years to Joe. After her divorce, Jane dated a number of men, and then one evening met Cynthia at a party. Much to her amazement, Jane found that she was sexually attracted to Cynthia, who was a lesbian. Jane's situation is unusual because she was for the most part unaware of being attracted to females up until she met Cynthia. In looking back, Jane does remember having big crushes on other girls and feeling jealous of the time they spent with their boyfriends. Although these are normal feelings for teenagers to have, Jane feels she suffered more than other girls from these feelings of jealousy.

Jane and Cynthia began dating and having sex, and fell deeply in love with one another. Within a few months Cynthia moved in with Jane, and that's when the trouble began. Jane's three teenagers were unaware their mother had become a lesbian until Cynthia moved in. The kids were faced with two enormous issues at once: their mother was gay, and her lover was their new "sort of stepparent." Needless to say, the kids were furious.

Because the kids did not understand or like Jane's switch from straight to lesbian, they blamed Cynthia for bringing about this ugly change in their mother. The kids were convinced that if Cynthia had never come along their mother would still be "normal." Although Jane's kids are beginning to understand that their mother would have come out as a lesbian sooner or later, they still find it easier to be angry with Cynthia than with their own mother. For months they wouldn't even talk to Cynthia. They gradually allowed her to become somewhat friendly with them, but they still give her a lot of flak.

If you feel angry at your mom's or dad's lover, that's perfectly normal, but your anger is misdirected. Try to keep in mind that your parent's lover is not responsible for your parent coming out as being gay. It was your parent's own decision.

This adjustment may be more difficult for you if it was the parent of the same sex as you who chose to live as a gay. This is because you use that parent as a model and will feel very betrayed when the person whose sexuality you are copying seems to switch gears on you. Jane's two boys adjusted to her change somewhat more easily than did her daughter, Amy. Amy still feels very angry at Jane and hates Cynthia. She has become very close to a girlfriend's mother and seems to need to use her as a model right now until she becomes comfortable with her own sexuality.

Telling Your Parent How You Feel

When you become clear that it is really your parent and not the gay lover that you're maddest at, the next step is to begin talking to your parent about how you feel. Your parent may be uncomfortable with your anger but will be glad you're getting it off your chest and being honest about it. The anger you feel at your parent for being gay most likely won't go away quickly, especially if you just talk about it once. It's a good idea, then, to bring it up almost every time you feel it. If you talk about it often enough and long enough, your anger will decrease and you'll be able to live with the situation a little more easily. Your parent has had to do a great deal of self-examination throughout this crisis, and will probably understand your anger about their situation, so don't be afraid you'll hurt his or her feelings. Your parent wants what's best for you, and, short of living as a heterosexual again, will do whatever possible to help you adjust to this difficult situation.

Will I Be Gay, Too?

One of the scariest aspects of having a gay parent is the worry that you may be gay too. After all, it happened to your parent, what's to prevent the same thing from happening to you? Since we know and like gay people, being gay doesn't sound like the end of the world to us, but we know the idea may be very upsetting to you.

First, studies have shown that gay parents rarely have gay kids. Since we said "rarely," you're probably thinking, "Oh, no! Then there is a small chance that it might happen to me!" To clear up this concern, let's first discuss sexuality in general.

Practically every human being alive at this moment has had, at one time or another, some slight or strong sexual feelings about a person of the same sex. That's because people are not absolutely and always every minute either gay or straight, but rather fall on a continuum between heterosexual and homosexual. The vast majority of people are straight (about 90 percent) but still have sexual feelings toward someone of the same sex once in a while. At

the other end of the continuum are people who are homosexual, but who have felt attraction for the opposite sex
one or more times. People in the middle, bisexuals, are attracted to both sexes about equally.

It is also true that in the beginning of adolescence kids
often go through a time when they're attracted to the same
sex. You may remember having a "crush" on a teacher,
camp counselor, or friend of the same sex, although you
probably weren't aware that your feelings were sexual.
You just liked them a lot and wanted to be with them. This
does not mean you are gay, it is simply a stage of development. Most kids grow out of it and start developing feelings toward the opposite sex. About one third of all men, in
fact, have had at least one homosexual experience in their
lives, usually as an adolescent, but the vast majority of
these men end up as heterosexuals.

Most gay people know from an early age that they are
homosexuals. So, to figure out where you are on this issue,
you can try to check in with yourself. If you're really honest with yourself, you know whether or not you are attracted more to girls or boys. That will not change for you
as you grow older. In most parents' situation, it was probably much too scary to admit to themselves and the world
that they were gay, so they pretended to be straight. After
many years had passed they got tired of pretending and
said to their kids and others, "This is who I really am." If
your self-inventory tells you you are straight, then relax.
You're not going to change the way your parent has. If
you're gay, then you're lucky to have a parent who will understand and be supportive. If you are totally confused,
perhaps it would help to talk to a counselor about these
feelings.

What Do I Tell My Friends?

Jane's kids had a lot of trouble with this issue. They were
horribly embarrassed about their mother being gay and

(137)

didn't want anyone to know. Jane described it this way: "When I came out of the closet, my kids went in." They tried to avoid having their friends come over to their house so the kids wouldn't figure out what Cynthia was doing living here. After a while that got awkward and Jane's kids slowly began bringing friends home, but they were still very nervous. Eventually, all three told one or two close friends, but they don't want to talk about it much outside the family. Some other kids found out and treated them with some cruelty, so they had to start weeding out who their friends really were and spend time with the people who could support them.

When you are ready to talk, it will be a relief if you are able to tell a good friend, but there is unfortunately always the risk they will tell someone else, even though you swear them to secrecy. So, be very careful whom you tell if you don't want it spread around your school. As you start to feel okay about your parent being gay, then you will be more relaxed about telling the truth.

What to Do About Your Other Parent

Adults react to the news that an ex-spouse is gay in a variety of ways. Some feel relief, because they had an idea their spouse was gay but they were not quite sure. Some are a little surprised, but basically indifferent, while others get very mad. He or she may express anger to you by calling your gay parent names and not wanting you to live with, or even see, her or him. This is very painful for you because, although you may be angry, you still love your gay parent. You can't divorce a mom or dad emotionally the way their ex-spouse is doing. You need to assert yourself to your straight parent, and say firmly that it is too painful for you to hear negative talk about your gay parent. You have the right to ask that your feelings be respected by there being no destructive talk about your gay mom or dad in front of you.

When Am I Going to Stop Feeling So Upset?

It takes most teenagers a long time to get adjusted to having a parent who has recently disclosed they are gay. Most big changes take a long time to get used to. For instance, it takes people in a stepfamily three to five years to get used to one another and consolidate as a family, so it might take you about the same amount of time to grow accustomed to your parent's homosexuality.

If you are feeling very depressed, sometimes suicidal, very angry, withdrawing from your friends, starting to use drugs heavily or drinking a lot because you're so upset, then it's time to talk to someone fast about the problems you're having adjusting. (See Appendix III, "When to Get Professional Help.")

15 * What Is So Great About Stepfamilies?

A lot is terrific about stepfamilies! Sure there are a lot of problems, and that's what we have been focusing on throughout most of this book. We think it's important, in concluding, to recognize all the positive things that can happen to people and to relationships as a result of living in a stepfamily. In fact, when the workings of stepfamilies are understood, and when the relationships and feelings are dealt with openly and constructively, stepfamilies can be wonderfully successful and very healthy places in which to grow and live.

We believe that children in stepfamilies mature more quickly and learn more realistically about relationships. If you have two sets of parents and spend time in two different homes, you are naturally going to learn to learn different values and attitudes. Dealing with differences in an accepting way is very difficult for those of us who grew up in just one family. We learned that there is only one way to do things; our family's way is the "right" way. You have had to learn that there are many different ways of doing things and they are not right or wrong, they are just different. There is no way to convey to you how important this lesson will be to you in your adult life. Adults in therapy sometimes take months and years to learn that kind of tolerance and acceptance.

If both your parents are remarried, you have four adults available to you, and if you have fairly good relationships with all those adults, you can get a lot more needs met than other kids. It's sort of like the old "extended family" where Grandma and Grandpa lived around the corner, and aunts and uncles and cousins lived on neighboring farms or up the street. You may have one parent who is really good at listening to problems and helping you that way, another who is good at helping you with algebra, another who makes fantastic cookies, and another who loves to hug you or take you special places. You have the opportunity to learn a great variety of skills, whether cooking, changing the oil in a car, or using a computer. Many kids tell us that their stepparent is a much more objective listener when talking about colleges, careers, sex, or whatever, because he or she is less emotionally involved with you and doesn't overreact when you express your ideas.

Besides having the opportunity to relate to and learn from more adults, you have the opportunity to form good friendships with your stepbrothers and stepsisters too. We know this is rough going at first, or it may seem as though you have nothing in common, but as adults, it is very special to have relatives nearby to spend holidays and other family times with. Those stepbrothers and stepsisters can be very close friends for life if you give your relationships a chance.

There are also many advantages to living with adults who are in their second marriage, although we're sure you have never thought of it that way before. You have been busy wishing your natural parents were still together, but it is important to remember how it was when they were together before the divorce. There was probably a lot of tension, conflict, or, at best, a lot of distance between them. That situation was not very good modeling for you as a growing person. Almost everything you learn about how to get along with a husband or wife you learn from watching your parents relate to each other. What you learned from your real parents at the end of their relationship was how *not* to get along in marriage. You deserve a chance to live with adults who love each other a lot, and who have made a more mature choice than they did the first time around (or at least, we hope they have). They are probably more affectionate than your real parents were, more considerate of each other, and in general, they are probably providing a better lesson for you in how to have a good marriage. Even if you are not aware of this happening, or if you are so resentful of your stepparent that you cannot appreciate their relationship, you are still learning from it. Usually adults in a second marriage have more flexible roles than before. They often divide up household chores in a more equal way and are not stuck in their "traditional" male/female roles quite so much. So your education in living together equally will provide you with better resources for having a more equal relationship yourself when you are married.

There is some evidence that children from stepfamilies form better relationships as adults than other people do. Because of the severity of the problems in stepfamilies, they have learned to communicate about problems and resolve them. You are probably not going to be content as an adult to sweep your problems under the rug and talk about the weather.

The stepfamily is a courageous and positive new family unit. It is *not* second-class. We will soon be in the majority, in fact. We are a different kind of family and we face different kinds of problems than other families. But we will survive and provide a second chance of happiness for millions of adults and children.

Appendix I. How to Hold a Family Council

A good way for stepfamilies to resolve differences and problems and to keep the family running smoothly is to hold family councils on a regular basis. There are no rigid rules to follow since you have to do what fits your family the best. Here are some guidelines, however, that will help you get started.

Choose a table where each member of the family can pull up a chair. We have found that sitting around a table works better than lounging around the living room. Include everyone who is living in your house at the time, especially visiting stepchildren. Provide a notebook and pencil to make a permanent record of the decisions reached.

Choose a chairperson to run the meeting and a secretary to write down any decisions made. Rotate chairperson and secretary every meeting or every month. Be sure to decide at each meeting who will chair the next one, so that person can be responsible for making sure the next meeting happens.

Use your first meeting to explain about family meetings and what they will be used for. Read our suggestions aloud, if you like, and decide how often and when the family wants to have meetings. You might try to talk about just one issue, like welcoming a stepchild for a visit, planning something for the family to do together, or scheduling a complicated weekend. Keep the first meeting short, no longer than fifteen minutes, and try to keep the discussion positive. Have everyone save their grievances or problems for another meeting.

Plan something fun for after the meeting, especially the first meeting, like going out for ice cream or playing a favorite family card game. You could have your chairperson, or secretary, or both, be responsible for serving refreshments after the meeting.

You may need to spend one whole meeting working out jobs and allowances if these areas are not working well in your family. Mom and Dad will probably be able to provide a list of the household chores that they need help with. Then let everyone participate in choosing the jobs they are willing to take responsibility for. We have found that jobs work best if they are on a rotating basis.

One method that works well for one stepfamily is to keep three cards (because there are three children) on the refrigerator listing two or three jobs for each child on each card. Every Saturday the cards change and the kids take on different jobs for the next week. This family has alternate sets of four and five cards, so that when stepchildren are visiting for more than a weekend, they have regular jobs to do also.

We also suggest that allowances not be connected directly to jobs done. That becomes too complicated and Mom or Dad becomes the "boss"—not a comfortable position, especially for a stepparent. We feel that everyone who is living in a family deserves to share in some of the money, *and* they need to share in the responsibilities. Instead of withholding allowances, decide at a family meeting what to do when people are not doing their jobs. Try to think of a logical consequence: if Joe doesn't set the table, then everyone sets his or her own place and helps with the food, but Joe doesn't get to eat with the family. (You can allow him to fix his own food later and clean it up if you want to.)

An agenda may be followed at each meeting. It could

Week 1

Ken	Roz	Rick
Feed animals	Set table & help prepare meals	Clear table & help cleanup
Garbage & wastebaskets	Keep family room picked up & cleaned	Keep bathroom clean

Week 2

Ken	Roz	Rick
Clean up	Animals	Set table
Bathroom	Garbage	Family room

Week 3

Ken	Roz	Rick
Set table	Clean up	Animals
Family room	Bathroom	Garbage

be posted during the week and available for everyone to write down items they wish to discuss.

A possible agenda might be:

- Reading of minutes from previous meeting
- Calendar for coming week
- Bank and other financial transactions
- Old business
- New business
- Future plans

Do not allow the family meeting to become just a time for talking about jobs and petty grievances. A grievance can be brought up by any family member, however, and the chairperson can act as a mediator to help two people listen to each other and try to work out their problem. Parents should try not to sermonize, moralize, or run the meeting. They get to state any problem they are having like everyone else, of course.

Handling grievances and conflicts will work best if you follow these rules:

1. Grievances must be stated as an "I message," not an attack on another person. (See Chapter 2, "How to Talk to a Stepparent," for what an "I message" is.)

2. Have members speak directly to each other. "I feel upset when I find your hair in my hairbrush," rather than "She always uses my stuff."

3. No interrupting. Everyone has the right to speak his or her thoughts and finish before another person speaks.

4. No put-downs, sarcastic comments, or swearing.

5. If someone gets too upset and wants to leave the meeting, adjourn until another time.

If you have a vacation or holiday coming up, the family as a group can plan for this. Those family meetings are the most fun.

Another idea for teaching family members how to share and to keep the meeting positive is to begin by having everyone share the best thing that happened to them during the week, the most embarrassing thing that happened, or what they like best about one other person in the family.

Holding a family council is not always easy, but as you go week to week, you will find that your family will look forward to these times for joint thought and action. Tension and conflict in your house will be reduced as people learn to resolve their differences in the family meeting. Everyone can learn better ways of communicating and listening to each other, and often come to enjoy one another more as people.

Appendix II. Nine Ways for Stepparents and Stepkids to Become Friends

Some recent studies have taught us that stepfamilies consider themselves "happy" when the stepparents and stepchildren have become friends!* In these families, the stepparent has used certain strategies to try to be friends with his or her stepchildren, and has continued to try again even after being rejected at first by the stepchild. Stepparents and stepkids report "liking" one another when a majority of these strategies are in operation. We feel that teenagers as well as stepparents can initiate some of these ways of getting together.

* "Nine Ways For Stepparents and Stepkids to Become Friends" adapted from "Affiliating in Stepfather Families: Teachable Strategies Leading to Stepfather-Child Friendship," by Phyllis Noerager Stern, *Western Journal of Nursing Research*, 1982, Vol. 4, No. 1.

1. Spend Time Alone

Friendships usually only develop in a one-on-one interaction. It is difficult for a very good relationship to develop as long as the natural parent or other children are around. Family togetherness is fine, but stepparents and stepchildren need alone time together. Both teenagers and parents can invite each other to come along for errands or other activities.

2. Good Timing

Stepkids need some time to adjust to the household before and after a visit or telephone conversation with their other parent. Likewise, stepkids should back off a little when their stepparent's natural children are around. This is a delicate time when loyalty conflicts are most likely to occur. Stepparents need to be careful not to come on too strong or push a stepchild into a relationship too fast. Both stepparents and stepkids can learn to respect each other's "not so good" moods.

Another important act of friendship and timing can be saying the right thing at the right time to bolster the other's self-esteem. A stepparent or a stepchild can acknowledge a job well done, an act of kindness or consideration, a witty comment, or the other's physical appearance. A well-timed compliment goes a long way toward developing a friendship.

3. Spending Money

Whether we like it or not, money and material things represent love, giving, and being a member of the family. Teenage stepkids are old enough to be told whose money goes where, so that they understand that their stepparent is contributing to their support. Sometimes a simple change, such as the stepparent rather than the natural parent giving out allowances, can be a significant act of sharing. Stepparents can demonstrate their generosity by digging in their pocket or purse for a quarter for gum or a video game, or for sponsoring the trip to the shoe store for a new pair of tennies.

From a stepchild's point of view, a stranger joining his or her family is intrusion enough, but being stingy after arriving makes the intrusion unforgivable.

4. Teaching Skills

Adults have lots of skills and talents, and sharing these provides a nice opportunity for parent-child bonding. Whether it's baking a favorite dessert, changing the oil in the car, framing a picture, or playing golf, kids are usually receptive to watching and learning. Often stepparents are a bit more objective and more patient as teachers than are natural parents. Stepkids can easily initiate these activities by asking or just showing up and watching or asking questions.

On the other hand, close supervision, or following a child around to make sure a job is done properly, has been found to be detrimental to the developing friendship.

5. Coming Through In An Emergency

We can't necessarily arrange an emergency, but they seem to occur often enough on their own. This is a good opportunity for a stepparent to step in and drive to the emergency room, to the vet's, or go to pick up a child who's stranded somewhere. Stepkids can initiate some of this interaction by calling the stepparent at work with a problem, rather than always relying on the natural parent.

6. "Leveling" (Being Honest)

Leveling means telling the other person how his or her behavior affects you. This is different from discipline, which we usually recommend that the stepparent not try to do right away. Leveling means keeping feelings out in the open so that they don't build up and get in the way of stepparent and child liking each other. Leveling means saying, "Please stop kicking my chair, it's making me crazy," rather than actually going crazy inside. It means saying, "It really bothers me when you use that tone of voice with your mother," rather than thinking the kid is rude, snotty, and no good.

For teenagers, leveling means saying, "I hate it when you give me that look. I would rather have you tell me what's bothering you," or, "Please don't tease me about my girlfriend. That really embarrasses me." (See Chapter 2, "How to Talk to a Stepparent.")

7. Developing Trust; Keeping Promises

We all learn to like each other more quickly if we remember to make only promises that we can keep. Kids are especially vulnerable to disappointment when they have been looking forward to something fun. Adults sometimes put off the promised movie or shopping trip because they are busy, without realizing how important that plan is to a kid. Developing trust also means not revealing a thought or a feeling told in confidence or overheard, and not teasing about sensitive issues.

8. Accepting The Child The Way He or She Is

By the time a child is a teenager, his or her values, ideas, personality, and temperament are pretty well established. Stepparents need to accept that they can't change

(151)

or reform a child. They also need to remind themselves that they probably don't get to see the best part of that child; many teenagers are only their best, grown-up selves with their friends or at school. At home they are sometimes their most childish, unattractive selves. A stepparent can certainly influence a child, but change begins with accepting the person as he or she is, then proceeds by modeling values you would like to see develop, and by negotiating for changes in behavior that affect you directly. Stepkids need to accept the fact that traits they don't like in their stepparent are probably not going to change, either.

9. Realigning

"Realigning" is a fancy word for sticking up for a stepchild or a stepparent who is under fire from someone else. It means being an advocate for a child who is being attacked by his or her stepsiblings or disciplined harshly by his or her natural parent. It is not a good idea to contradict or sabotage the natural parent who is trying to discipline, but you could approach your spouse privately and say, "I would be comfortable letting her go to the party as long as we have the phone number." You can also approach the child privately and say, "I'm sorry this didn't work out for you. Is there anything I can do to help?"

Appendix III. When To Get Professional Help

Getting through your teen years is no easy task in this culture, and we feel that most teenagers and their families could benefit by occasional professional help. Stepfamilies, in particular, have a very difficult time putting their family together without some kind of educational or therapeutic help. Unfortunately, there is still somewhat of a stigma about seeing a psychologist or other family counselor, and many people are not comfortable talking to someone outside their family.

If you broke your arm or had a sore throat, your parents would not hesitate to take you to the doctor. If you are not happy, or if something is bothering you, we would hope that your mom or dad would find a qualified therapist for you to talk with. Many teenagers are asking their parents to find them help, and when they come in for counseling, they seem to know that talking about their problem may help them to get it sorted out and look at some things they could do to feel better. Don't be afraid to ask for the help you need, no matter how silly your problem may seem. Usually teenagers' problems get worse, not better, and the longer you wait to get help, the longer it takes for us to help you deal with the problem. Most of the teenagers and stepfamilies we see should have come for help earlier. By the time they call a counselor, they are in a crisis or things at home are awful.

When you are in a stepfamily, it is very important that you find a therapist who is trained in stepfamily dynamics and is experienced in working with stepfamilies. There are many differences between stepfamilies and intact families, as you know, and a therapist needs to understand those differences.

Although you may want to talk to a therapist for many reasons of your own, we have made a list of problems that teenagers have that are symptoms of a serious difficulty. If you find yourself on the list, you should try to arrange to get some professional help.

1. Depression

If you are frequently depressed, sad, and feel miserable all the time, you are in need of help. A teen who is withdrawn, doesn't see friends, and has no energy also may be depressed.

2. Suicidal Thoughts

If you feel like life is not worth living and start to think about ways to do away with yourself, even if just to get even with your parents, you need help immediately. If you hear a friend talk about killing him- or herself and saying that life is hopeless, tell the person's parents so they can get help for their child. There is an alarming number of adolescent suicides. We don't want to lose you!

3. Drugs and Alcohol

If you are drinking more than occasionally, or drinking occasionally to the point where you have lost control over your behavior, or if you are smoking pot more than occasionally, you need to talk with someone about it. If you are involved with any other drugs at all, it would be good to talk to a therapist and evaluate what kind of a life-style you are developing. A therapist won't judge you or turn you in, but will help you look at other ways to make yourself happy or to cope with problems other than tuning out.

4. Failing in School

If you are getting lousy grades, hating school, cutting classes, or getting in trouble by acting up in school, you need someone to help you evaluate what's going on.

5. Trouble With the Law

If you are shoplifting, burglarizing homes, stealing money from your parents, doing vandalism, or even getting too many traffic tickets or having accidents, you are definitely on the wrong track. An objective profes-sional can help you learn to take better care of yourself.

6. Being Sexually Unselective

If you are a girl sleeping around as a way of getting dates or of getting some warmth and love from other hu-man beings, you are not using your sexuality in a healthy way. If you are a boy and sleeping around so that you can claim more conquests, you are not learning to relate to women in a way that will lead to warm, healthy, mature relationships with them.

7. Having No Friends or Changing Friends

If you are withdrawn, have no friends, or have lost your friends, there is something wrong. If you give up your old friends and are involved with a new group of friends for the excitement value, that could be a sign that you are not as happy as you deserve to be with your life.

8. Hating Yourself

If you are constantly putting yourself down, letting other people take advantage of you, feeling that everything is your fault, feeling that you are stupid or worthless, you need help with your self-esteem. A therapist can help you to learn to like yourself better and be more assertive with other people.

9. Being Sexually or Physically Abused

If you are being sexually molested by anyone older than you, or being physically abused by your parent or stepparent, seeing a therapist can help you figure out what to do about this problem. If you can't ask your parents to get you to a therapist because of the circumstances, you can call a county mental health agency and find out where to get free help.

10. Too Much Conflict at Home

If your home is a war zone and you can't stand being there, whether or not you are directly involved with the conflict, a therapist will help you learn to cope with what is going on. A therapist also may be able to get your parents to come in if you begin by asking for help for yourself.

11. Having A Parent Who Is Alcoholic Or Abusing Drugs

Any teenager who lives with a drug problem at home needs special help to learn how to get removed from the problem and learn to grow in a healthful way. It is easy to get into the role of taking care of a parent who has this kind of a problem, or to help the other parent be a "policeman" around the house. This role is *not* in your best interest and you need to learn how to divorce yourself from the problem and begin living your own life.

12. Sudden Weight Loss or Weight Gain

If you are constantly worried about being too fat and are starving yourself or throwing up, you need help immediately! If you are obese and eat to make yourself feel better, you had best get yourself to a therapist, also. These problems need to be taken care of early so that they don't develop in to a serious health problem.

Appendix IV. Books of Interest for Stepfamilies

For Stepchildren

Berman, Claire. *What Am I Doing In a Stepfamily?* Secaucus, NJ: Lyle Stuart, Inc., 1982.

Bradley, Buff. *Where Do I Belong? A Kid's Guide to Stepfamilies.* Reading, MA: Addison-Wesley, 1982.

Burt, Mala Schuster, and Burt, Roger B. *What's Special About Our Stepfamily: A Participation Book for Children.* New York: Doubleday, 1983.

Byars, Betsy. *The Animal, the Vegetable and John D. Jones.* New York: Delacorte, 1982.

Clifton, Lucille. *Everett Anderson's Nine Months Long.* New York: Holt, Rinehart & Winston, 1978.

Craven, Linda. *Stepfamilies: New Patterns in Harmony.* New York: Julian Messner, 1982.

Gardner, Richard A. *The Boys and Girls Book About Divorce: With An Introduction For Parents.* New York: Bantam Edition, 1971.

———. *The Boys and Girls Book About Stepfamilies.* New York: Bantam Books, 1982.

Green, Phyllis. *A New Mother For Martha.* New York: Human Sciences Press, 1978.

Hunter, Evan. *Me and Mr. Stenner.* New York: J.B. Lippincott, 1976.

LeShan, Eda J. *What's Going to Happen to Me? When Parents Separate or Divorce.* Four Winds Press, 1978.

Lewis, Helen Coale. *All About Families—The Second Time Around.* Atlanta: Peachtree Publishers, 1980.

Pevsner, Stella. *A Smart Kid Like You.* New York: Seabury Press, 1976.

Sobol, Harriet. *My Other Mother, My Other Father.* New York: Macmillan, 1979.

Stenson, Janet Sinberg. *Now I Have a Stepparent and It's Kind of Confusing.* New York: Avon, 1980.

Wolitzer, Hilma. *Out of Love.* New York: Farrar, Straus & Giroux, 1976.

For Parents and Stepparents

Atkin, Edith, and Rubin, Estelle. *Part-Time Father.* New York: Signet Edition, 1977.

Bayard, Robert T., and Bayard, Jean. *How to Deal with Your Acting-Up Teenager—Practical Self-Help for Desperate Parents.* San Jose, CA: The Accord Press, 1981.

Berman, Claire. *Making it as a Stepparent: New Roles/New Rules.* New York: Doubleday, 1980.

Einstein, Elizabeth. *The Stepfamily: Living, Loving and Learning.* New York: Macmillan, 1982.

Maddox, Brenda. *The Half-Parent.* New York: Evans, 1975.

Mayleas, Davidyne. *Re-wedded Bliss: Love, Alimony, Incest, Ex-spouse and Other Domestic Blessings.* New York: Basic Books, 1977.

Noble, June, and Noble, William. *How to Live With Other People's Children.* New York: Hawthorne Books, 1977.

Reingold, Carmel Berman. *Remarriage.* New York: Harper & Row, 1976.

Ricci, Isolina. *Mom's House, Dad's House: Making Shared Custody Work.* New York, Macmillan, 1980.

Roosevelt, Ruth, and Lofas, Jeanette. *Living in Step.* New York: Stein & Day, 1976.

Rosenbaum, Jean, and Rosenbaum, Veryl. *Stepparenting.*

Corte Madera, California: Chandler and Sharp Publishers, Inc. 1977.

Satir, Virginia. *Peoplemaking*. Palo Alto, California: Science and Behavior Books, Inc., 1972.

Simon, Anne W. *Stepchild in the Family: A View of Children in Remarriage*. New York: Odyssey Press, 1964.

Spann, Owen, and Spann, Nancie. *Your Child? I Thought it Was My Child!* Pasadena, California: Ward Ritchie Press, 1977.

Thayer, Nancy. *Stepping*. New York: Doubleday, 1980.

Thomson, Helen. *The Successful Stepparent*. New York: Harper and Row, 1966.

Westoff, Leslie Aldridge. *The Second Time Around: Remarriage in America*. New York: Viking, 1975.

Visher, Emily, and Visher, John. *Stepfamilies: Myths and Realities*. Secaucus, NJ: Citadel Press, 1980.

———. *How to Win as a Stepfamily*. New York: Dembner Books, 1982.

Wallerstein, Judith, and Kelly, Joan. *Surviving the Breakup*. New York: Basic Books, Inc., 1980.

Appendix V. About The Stepfamily Association of America

Why An Organization?

All families need information, education, and support. This is especially true for the stepfamily, which faces special challenges. The role of the stepparent differs from that of the biological parent—although society often sees the two as one and the same. A remarried parent deals with different issues than the parent in a first marriage. Stepchildren, too, find themselves coping with a variety of complex relationships. While informational, educational, and supportive services are available for biologic families, they fail to address the unique differences within the stepfamily. These include:

• A stepfamily is born of many losses.
• Family members have different histories and expectations.
• Parent-child relationships predate the relationship of the new couple.
• An influential biological parent exists elsewhere in actuality or in memory.
• Children may be members of two or more households.
• Legal relationships are ambiguous or nonexistent.

What Does The Association Do?

The Stepfamily Association of America, Inc., is a nonprofit organization that acts as a support network and national advocate for stepparents, remarried parents, and their children. Their goal is to improve the quality of life for millions of American stepfamilies and affirm the value of step relationships.

Although stepfamilies face distinct challenges, we should not lose sight of the richness and rewards to be found in reunification and recommitment. The Association is dedicated to helping the community and members of stepfamilies understand and deal with the differences in positive ways that bring satisfaction and a sense of personal growth and accomplishment.

Membership Entitles You To:

- *Stepfamily Bulletin,* a quarterly publication that includes feature articles, book reviews, up-to-date reports on studies and events that affect the stepfamily, a children's section, and news of the Stepfamily Association network.
- Informational Materials of interest to stepfamilies, including book lists, helpful guidelines, and information about the Association and its activities.
- Membership in affiliated state divisions and affiliated chapters where they exist. Local chapters provide educational and social activities and support groups.
- Reduced registration fee for annual membership conference and state and local conferences.
- Discount on books, etc., sold by the Association Sales Program.

Community Education

The importance of educating the community to the reality of stepfamily living cannot be overstressed. The Association accomplishes this by various means, including:

• Publications. In addition to the *Bulletin*, the Association publishes an up-to-date bibiliography of books, articles, and research reports having to do with the stepfamily.

• Public information. The Association encourages greater media coverage of this form of family formation, providing accurate information on stepfamily dynamics and programs.

• Workshops. The Association recommends qualified speakers and workshop leaders for professional and lay audiences.

Professional Training

Agencies, clinics, schools, and churches, as well as individual educators, attorneys, therapists, and counselors, are seeking to increase the effectiveness of their services and programs for individuals in stepfamilies. They provide professionals trained by the Association to lead workshops and in-service training programs for such groups. The Association maintains a resource list of interested educators, social group workers, and mental health practitioners who have participated in an approved two-day professional workshop dealing with stepfamily issues. Names on this resource list are sent to the appropriate state division or affiliated chapter, or are available on request where no state division or chapter exists.

Division and Chapter Development

A list of affiliated state divisions and affiliated chapters is available upon written request. Members interested in starting divisions or chapters are urged to contact the National Office for organizational information.

Research

The Association is engaged in research directed toward increasing our knowledge regarding successful ways of dealing with stepfamily situations. They publish a list of references for researchers in this field of interest, and they work cooperatively with responsible persons and organizations engaged in learning more about stepfamily issues, including the effect of cultural attitudes toward the remarried family in which at least one partner has had a child in a previous relationship.

For Membership Information Contact:

Stepfamily Association of America, Inc.
28 Allegheny Avenue, Suite 1307
Baltimore, MD 21204

INDEX

INDEX

Abuse, *see* Physical abuse; Sexual abuse
Affection, stepmothers' excesses of, 54–55
Aggressiveness, teenagers' messages containing, 13–15
Alcohol, teenagers' use of, 154–55
Alcoholism, parents with, teenagers' feelings about, 98–99, 156–57
Allowances, 144
Anger
  of stepmothers, 46
  of teenagers, 10–11, 134–36
Arguments, 40–41, 113–15
Assertiveness, relationships improved with, 15–21

Biological parents
  absence of one, 93–102
  alcoholism in, 98–99, 156–57
  competition with stepparents by, 39, 63–64
  death of, 100–1
  homosexuality in, 132–39
  hostility between, 89, 94–95
  mental illness in, 98–99
  new marriages of, 30–31
  self-centeredness of, 97–98
  sexuality of, 118–20
  stepsiblings and, 104–12

teenagers' attempts to reunite, 24–26
  visiting with, 80–92
Borrowing, 38, 39
Brothers, *see* Siblings

Child abuse, *see* Physical abuse; Sexual abuse
Chores, delegating responsibility for, 144–45
Cleanliness, 38–39, 40
  stepmothers' obsessions with, 52–54
Communication with stepparents, 13–21, 143–47
Competition between stepparents and biological parents, 39, 63–64
Cooking, criticizing of stepmothers', 37
Counseling, professional, 153–57

Death, 100–1
Depression, 154
Dictatorial behavior of stepfathers, 68–70
Disloyalty, teenagers' feelings of, 86–87
Divorce, effects on teenagers of, 22–27
Drugs
  parents' use of, 156–57
  teenagers' use of, 154–55

Emergencies, stepchildren-
stepparent interaction
initiated during, 150
Emotions, *see* Feelings
Families, withdrawal from, 9
Family council, how to hold,
143-47
Favoritism by stepmothers,
57-58
Feelings
expressing of, 13-21
of stepfathers
guilt, 64-66
jealousy, 62-63
of stepmothers
anger, 46
jealousy, 46-47
of teenagers
anger, 10-11, 134-36
about being unloved, 30
depression, 154
disloyalty, 86-87
about divorce, 22-27
about homosexuality,
136-39
guilt, 86-87
moodiness, 9-10
self-hatred, 156
sexual, 112-13, 121-24,
128-31
suicidal, 154
Food, stepmothers' gripes con-
cerning, 37, 38
Friends
lack of, 155-56
teenagers' desire to be with,
8-9
Greeting stepmothers, teenagers' forgetfulness in,
38

Grouchiness of stepfathers,
70-72
Guilt feelings
of stepfathers, 64-66
of teenagers, 86-87
Homosexuality, 132-39
Honesty, 151
Hostility between parents, 89,
94-95
Indifference by stepfathers,
72-73
Jealousy
of stepfathers toward stepchildren, 62-63
of stepmothers toward stepchildren, 46-47
Law, trouble with, 155
Listening, as part of communication, 20-21
Love
of stepmothers for step-
children, 45
of teenagers for stepparents,
32-34
types of, 28-31
Marriage, *see* Remarriage
Mental illness, parents with,
teenagers' feelings
about, 98-99
Messiness, 38-39, 40
stepmothers' obsessions
with, 52-54
Messenger, parents using teenagers as, 89
Money
sharing and, 149-50

stepfathers' feelings about,
66–67
Moodiness, teenagers' swings
of, 9–10

Names for stepparents, 34–36

Parents, *see* Biological parents;
Stepparents
Physical abuse, 78–79, 156
See also Sexual abuse
Privacy, teenagers' need for,
7–8, 149
Professional help, how to ob-
tain, 153–57
Promises, keeping of, 151

Rebelliousness, as natural
growth process, 5–7
Reform of teenagers, stepmothers' attempts at,
47–49
Rejection by stepmothers,
58–59
Relationships
with biological parents, 29,
80–92, 93–102
with friends, 8–9
improvement of, 50–60,
148–52
with stepfathers, 32–36
with stepmothers, 50–60
with stepsiblings, 103–16
Relatives
separation from, 101–2
step-, acceptance and rejection by, 41–42
Remarriage, 28–31, 120–21
Respectfulness, stepfathers' de-
sires for, 39
Responsibility

of stepmothers, 50–52
of teenagers, 40

School, failing in, 155
Self-hatred, teenagers' feelings
of, 156
Separation from siblings,
101–2
Sexual abuse, 73–75, 125–28,
156
See also Physical abuse
Sexuality
attraction in, 112–13, 121–24,
128–31
promiscuity in, 155
in stepfamily, 117–31
See also Homosexuality
Siblings
biological, separation from,
101–2
step-, 103–16
arguments with, 113–15
dislike of, 115–16
sexual attraction towards,
112–13, 128–31
Sisters, *see* Siblings
Skills, sharing of, 150
Sloppiness, 38–39, 40
stepmothers' obsessions
with, 52–54
Stepbrothers, *see* Siblings—
step
Stepfamilies
advantages of, 140–42
homosexuality in, 132–39
sexuality in, 117–31
Stepfathers
competitiveness with biological father by, 63–64
as dictators, 68–70
gripes of, 39–40

grouchiness of, 70–72
guilt feelings of, 64–66
happiness of, 79
indifference of, 72–73
invisibility of, 75–76
jealousy of, 62–63
money and, 66–67
without own children, 76–78
physical abuse by, 78–79
respect towards, 39
sexual abuse by, 73–75, 125–27
uncertainties of, 61–62
Stepgrandparents, acceptance of teenagers by, 41–42
Stepmothers
affection from, 54–55
anger of, 46
cleanliness and, 52–54
favoritism by, 57–58
greeting of, 38
gripes of, 37–39
happiness of, 59–60
improving relationships with, 50–60
jealousy of, 46–47
love by, 45
without own children, 55–57
rejection by, 58–59
responsibility of, 50–52
sexual abuse by, 127–28
teenagers' values and, 47–49
Stepparents
communicating with, 13–21
competition with biological parents by, 39, 63–64
homosexuality in, 132–39
improving relationships with, 148–52

love for, 32–34
names for, 34–36
pet peeves of, 36–37
sexual attraction towards, 121–24
Stepsisters, see Siblings—step
Suicidal feelings of teenagers, 154
Table manners, 38
Teenagers
aggressive messages of, 13–15
alcohol use by, 154–55
anger in, 10–11, 134–36
depression in, 154
divorce and, 22–27
drug use by, 154–55
feelings of being unloved of, 30
feelings of disloyalty in, 86–87
guilt feelings of, 86–87
love for stepparents by, 32–34
moodiness in, 9–10
privacy for, 7–8, 149
rebelliousness of, 5–7
reforming by stepmothers of, 47–49
responsibility in, 40
self-hatred in, 156
sexual feelings of, 112–13, 121–24, 128–31
suicidal feelings of, 154
values tested by, 11–12
Tidiness, 38–39, 40
stepmothers' obsessions with, 52–54
Trust, 151

Two homes, advantages of hav-
    ing, 92

Values
    stepmothers' attempts to
        change teenagers',
        47—49
    testing of, 11–12
Visitation to other parent's
    home, 80–92

Wastefulness, stepfather's
    gripes concerning,
    39–40
Weight, changes in, 157